Vinegar into Honey

Vinegar into Honey

SEVEN STEPS TO UNDERSTANDING AND TRANSFORMING ANGER, AGGRESSION, & VIOLENCE

Ron Leifer, M.D.

SNOW LION PUBLICATIONS
ITHACA, NEW YORK

Snow Lion Publications
P.O. Box 6483
Ithaca, NY 14851 USA
(607) 273-8519
www.snowlionpub.com

Printed in the USA on acid-free recycled paper.

ISBN-13: 978-1-55939-293-8
ISBN-10: 1-55939-293-2

Library of Congress Cataloging-in-Publication Data

Leifer, Ron, 1932-
Vinegar into honey : seven steps to understanding and
transforming anger, aggression, and violence / Ron Leifer.
    p. cm.
ISBN-13: 978-1-55939-293-8 (alk. paper)
ISBN-10: 1-55939-293-2 (alk. paper)
1. Buddhism—Psychology. 2. Anger—Religious aspects—
Buddhism. 3. Aggressiveness—Religious aspects—Buddhism.
4. Violence—Religious aspects—Buddhism.
  I. Title. BQ4570.P76L45 2008
294.3'4442—dc22
                                                    2008001964

Designed and typeset by Gopa & Ted2, Inc.

Table of Contents

In memory of Jamgon Kongtrul Rinpoche,
who predicted that Buddhism would come to America
through psychotherapy.

This book is dedicated to
Abria, Autumn, and Mandisa
and the children of their generation.

ACKNOWLEDGEMENTS

I am grateful to Rebecca Cutler for her tireless and meticulous editing of the manuscript, which has added eloquence, grace, and clarity to the text. She has been my most constructive critic and, as every writer and disciple knows, a loving critic is a most valuable teacher. Many thanks also to Liz Green, my editor at Snow Lion Publications, whose firm and skillful editing fine-tuned and improved the manuscript.

Preface

"Of the three fields of study the most important and especially pressing is the first which has to do with the stronger emotions; for a
strong emotion does not arise except when a desire fails to attain
its object, or when an aversion falls into what it would avoid. This is
the field of study which introduces to us confusions, tumults, misfor-
tunes and calamities; and sorrows, lamentations, envies . . . passions
which make it impossible for us even to listen to reason."
—EPICTETUS, *Discourses* 3.2.3

WHAT DO WE KNOW about anger, aggression, and violence? We
know a great deal about the physiology of anger, the psychology
of aggression, and the politics of violence. Biologists, psychologists, sociologists, philosophers, and theologians each have their
explanations and proposed solutions. But something is lacking
that weaves it all together into some fundamental understanding.
It may be that we have too many specialized explanations, a Tower
of Babel that prevents us from seeing what, after all, we may not
want to see.

"Vinegar into honey" is a Tibetan alchemical metaphor, like the
familiar European alchemical metaphor of turning lead into gold.
The literal meaning is not the inner meaning. Spiritual alchemy is
not the literal, chemical transformation of lead into gold. Its inner
meaning is the quest to transform unhappiness into happiness and
suffering into joy.

Vinegar into Honey is a seven-step manual for understanding and transforming the energy of anger, aggression, and violence into wisdom and inner peace. It calls for a journey within, an inquiry into ourselves—our hearts and minds. It is not a journey for the fainthearted. It can be an awesome, exhilarating adventure or a dark night of the soul, depending on how willing we are to see what we do not wish to see and to restrain ourselves from doing what we feel compelled to do.

The background of the views presented in this book derives from three principles that I adopted over years of difficult, painful searching for an understanding of my own suffering and the suffering of the people I see in my private psychotherapy office.

The first principle is that nothing human is alien—that is, that in some sense, the individual has part in the species and the species has part in the individual. Each of us possesses the potential to do anything any human has done. Each of us is vulnerable enough to experience anything any human has experienced. And each of us has the capacity for the wisdom and goodness that any human has achieved. The problems of anger, aggression, and violence must be approached without regarding them as "abnormal," as the emotions and actions of "others." In particular, I eschew the idea that they are mental illnesses or medical disorders. Instead, they are "normal" human emotions and behaviors, in that what we mean by normal is not "desirable" but "common," in which case we could claim, as some have, that the normal human mind is neurotic.

The second principle is to engage in a free-ranging inquiry across all branches of knowledge for a view of human nature and human suffering that makes sense and suggests a path of healing in tune with that sense. Psychoanalysis, psychology, anthropology, sociology, politics, religion, and literature all contain golden nuggets of wisdom. The view developed here is a bricolage, a patchwork of insights from here and facts from there. One cannot expect a final conclusion. Many wise people have been pondering this for centuries. Everyone has her own bricolage. The quest for knowledge is a continuous, open inquiry. This means that any inquiry, including this one, must necessarily be regarded as incomplete and tentative.

The third principle is more specific. It is based on the ancient and honored tradition of Buddhism. In search of a more profound understanding of the human condition than that provided by psychiatry, I turned to the wisdom of the East. My first teacher was Agehananda Bharati, a Hindu monk, Sanskrit scholar, and professor of anthropology at Syracuse University. In 1964, he introduced me to meditation and to a linguistic analysis of Hindu and Buddhist philosophy. In 1980, realizing that my curiosity was inclining towards Buddhism, he advised me to find a Buddhist teacher.

Seeking a teacher in 1980, I stumbled onto KTD, Karma Triyana Dharmachakra, a Tibetan Buddhist monastery in the Karma Kagyu tradition, located in Woodstock, New York. I asked if I could meet the Abbot. I was told by his translator, Ngodrup Burkhar, that I couldn't meet with him that day, but I could come to a teaching he was performing that night, "just to feel his presence." I had no idea what he meant by "presence" until I sat at the teaching and experienced him. I was fascinated by his calmness, sweetness, innocence, and wisdom. What state of mind is this? I had never heard of it in all my studies in medicine, psychiatry, philosophy, or the history of Western ideas.

I became a student of Khenpo Karthar Rinpoche, the abbot of the monastery. I attended his teachings and had irregular private meetings with him in the traditional guru-student relationship. I also attended the teachings and a few private meetings with some of the high lamas of the Kagyu tradition. At the time, the lamas were presenting very basic teachings to Westerners which were focused on the four noble truths, particularly on meditation and compassion. The lamas often said that "the Dharma is vast," meaning that the teachings themselves are as vast as the potential and the possibilities of the human experience of life. I didn't know what they meant at first, until I listened more and realized that these people, of this tradition, know more about human nature and the mind than anyone I had studied or knew of in Western society.

In 1986, Jamgon Kongtrul Rinpoche, one of the Kagyu regents, requested that a group of practitioners at the monastery who were mental health workers form a thousand-person conference on Buddhism and psychotherapy. He told us that he had a vision that Buddhism would come to the West, perhaps over decades or centuries, through psychotherapy. I had already been contemplating the similarities and differences between Buddhist and Western views on mental and emotional suffering. I have been practicing private psychotherapy now for more than forty-five years, seeing on average twenty persons a week—a rare, precious opportunity to explore the nature and causes of personal suffering.

I was particularly interested in the view of suffering presented in the first two noble truths, the fact of suffering and the causes of suffering. This view seemed natural and correct to me because of my life as a psychotherapist. Whatever their diagnosis is thought to be, my patients suffer and my responsibility is to help them find relief. I was curious to find a common ground of Buddhist and Western views on the problems of suffering and happiness. The fruit of this inquiry is my previous book, *The Happiness Project: Transforming the Three Poisons That Cause the Suffering We Inflict on Ourselves and Others* (Ithaca, Snow Lion Publications, 1997).

What are the "three poisons?" They are usually called passion, aggression, and ignorance or lust, hatred, and delusion. Each of these terms is semantically loaded and obscures the elegant simplicity of their meanings. The first two, passion and aggression, are an antithetical pair. They refer to an intrinsic quality of sentient life, bipolar reactivity—attraction and repulsion, moving towards and moving away from, desiring and avoiding. Primitive organisms are tropistic (trope = to turn). They turn towards light and life and move away from darkness and death. Higher organisms have developed simple and conditioned reflexes designed to promote life and well-being and to avoid danger and death. Western behavioral psychology has recognized this fundamental play of pain and pleasure, avoidance and attraction, as a key to understanding and controlling behavior. Freud expressed the same view in his idea of "the pleasure principle."

The terms "ignorance" and "delusion" refer to two kinds of "wrong thinking." "Ignorance" refers to the failure to see truths about ourselves and the nature of phenomena. "Delusion" means holding fixed, false ideas about them. The truths we fail to see are enumerated in the first noble truth as "the three facts of existence." These truths are (1) that suffering is a fact of life that cannot be completely avoided—we all suffer at birth, in sickness, in old age, and at death, and we all suffer from "normal neurotic mind"; (2) that we live in a sea of ceaseless change; nothing is permanent, not even the sun or the universe itself; and (3) that nothing, including ourselves, exists substantially—that is, in and of itself, separate from all the other energy transformations in the universe.

These facts expose ironies that most of us find difficult to comprehend because we suffer from our own habitual, contrary tendencies. Tragically, we seek happiness by struggling against the facts of existence. We want to avoid suffering and death that we cannot avoid. We want what we cannot have or what is harmful to ourselves or others. We hesitate to do what we must for our own benefit and that of others. We want our lives to be stable, constant, reliable, and under our control. We want to believe that our sense of ourselves is real, substantial, and important.

The fact of emptiness implies that our fixed, solid sense of ourselves, our personal identity, is a fiction which, by the magic of language, is transformed into a social "fact." Ignorance is the failure to see that our minds project desires, fears, and meanings onto ourselves and the world that we concretize and mistakenly take as "real." Delusion is the specific idea that we possess a substantial "self" that is the center of the universe, that our personal stories are hard reality, and that we should have things our own way. These facts are shattering because they reveal that we are the cause of our own suffering.

This book applies the principles of the three causes of suffering to the problems of anger, aggression, and violence. It is painful to contemplate the causes and cures of this predicament because they contradict the instinct for survival as it manifests in the assertion of personal, social, political, and national identity. Who is foolish enough to surrender their insatiable desires, to face their most dreaded fears, and to put others first for the sake of peace? The sad fact is that the desires and fears which energize human anger, aggression, and violence are more compelling than the desire for peace and harmony. As Shantideva said, "We shrink from suffering, but love its causes." Perhaps if we have a better understanding of our fundamental human nature and flaws, we may be better able to see how we cause suffering to ourselves and others, to discern the connection between our motives, our actions, and their consequences, and to act with the wisdom that is the mother of peace.

For those who wish to explore the path less traveled, this book is a seven-step approach to transforming the vinegar of anger, aggression, and violence into honey. "Honey" is a metaphor for a state which, while one cannot call it happiness as we ordinarily understand it, opens into a space of acceptance of the facts of life with inner equanimity and equilibrium. It is a state of openness to both the goodness and pain of life, and of sympathy for everyone, because we all live in the same human predicament.

I. The Mark of Cain

"... when they were in the field, Cain set upon his brother
Abel and killed him." —GENESIS 4:8

No ONE TODAY has to be reminded that human beings can be
angry, aggressive, and violent. Animals don't conduct warfare, seek
retribution, devise tactical terrors, or kill with a rationale. Only
humans do.

Violence is the great moral problem, the terrible riddle, the tragic
dilemma of human history. From the media attention it gets, we
might think that violence is increasing in our time. But it has been
this way since the beginning. Human violence appears in history
when humans appear.

All of human history is marked by the fires of aggression. Tribal,
ethnic, and religious groups have been fighting from prehistory to
the present. Cities were built as walled refuges against bandits and
marauders. For three centuries, Europe was lit by the fires of the
Inquisition. The twentieth century was bloodied by two world wars
and more than a hundred cruel conflicts since World War II, including Korea, Vietnam, Afghanistan, and now, at the dawn of the new
millennium, Iraq. Perhaps this world will end in a great final ges-
ture of human rage. Perhaps my life or yours will be undone by our
own or someone else's unchecked wrath. Why? What have we failed
to understand?

I don't mean, "What is the *particular* explanation for any *particular* act of violence?" Every violent actor has his or her own reasons.

The question is not why this particular person kills or why that particular nation attacks. We cannot hope to clarify the problem of human violence simply by enumerating a plethora of individual motives. We need to understand the *root cause* of aggression: Is there something about human nature that motivates us—all of us to some degree—to violence?

We are unaware of our lack of understanding *not* because we lack explanations for violence but because we have *too many* of them. We look to the various experts for answers and they see violence through the lenses of their own special disciplines, theories, and interests, presenting us with a veritable Tower of Babel. Psychiatrists, psychologists, sociologists, criminologists, economists, and politicians each have their own partial truths and their own language for expressing them.

If we ask psychiatrists to explain acts of violence they will tell us that the cause is mental illness. In their view, the violence is reduced to a genetic defect, a biochemical imbalance, or some other form of brain disease. In a kind of circular logic, if the perpetrator of a crime has ever seen a psychiatrist or been prescribed a psychiatric drug, it is taken as evidence of a biological cause. Biological factors surely play a part in anger, aggression, and violence, as they play a part in all human behavior. But what does this explain? How does this help us? Only psychiatrists pretend to understand "mental illness," and psychiatry is more a collegiality of opinions than a reliable science.

Sociologists and psychologists offer other explanations for anger, aggression, and violence. Sociologists usually claim that a violent child is a product of a dysfunctional family or school. Or, they blame a culture in which violence is commonplace and even valorized. Psychologists say a child becomes a killer because he was abused, ignored, deprived, indulged, repressed, bullied, insulted, or in some way traumatized at home or at school. Surely, these experiences are painful or traumatic. But not every child reared in a dysfunctional family or every victim of poverty, neglect, resentment, or abuse becomes violent. Why? In physics, causes always work. If you drop a stone from a bridge it doesn't sometimes fall and at other times fail to fall. Why do some people become violent under the same conditions in which others do not?

A culture in which violence is normative surely begets violence. A culture that accepts the exploitation of women promotes the exploitation of women. But not every man or woman who lives in such culture becomes an exploiter, an abuser, or a killer. Why some and not others?

Psychiatrists, psychologists, and social scientists explain this discrepancy as *caused* by genetic, hormonal, neurological, mental, or emotional "disorders" of the particular individual. They say that violence is caused by mental illness, or by a biochemical imbalance, or by a low tolerance for frustration, or by childhood traumas, or by social injustice. Few experts would dare explain the discrepancy as a moral failure although, ironically, many lay people would. Most social scientists and psychiatrists think this would "stigmatize" the violent individual who, they believe, is not responsible for his behavior since it is "caused." To acknowledge that many who inflict suffering have themselves suffered is compassionate, but does reducing the violent individual to a conditioned automaton explain or ameliorate the problem?

There are, basically, only two kinds of explanation of human action: causal and motivational, that is, determined and chosen. Causal explanations are partial truths, but they are only partial. Of course, biological and social factors play a part, and difficult people and unfavorable social conditions may provoke us. We all have our weaknesses, grievances, and wounds. But not everyone becomes violent. Why do some become violent and not others? This is the key question.

To avoid the confusion bred by this surplus of explanations we must expand our horizons and raise our gaze from the particular to the general, from the specific human individual or group to the human species itself. Do the roots of human anger, aggression, and violence lie in human nature? What would it mean to find the root causes of anger, aggression, and violence in human nature?

If we view humans as biological machines driven by genetics and brain biochemistry then extinguishing violence would have to be achieved by means of genetic engineering and drugs. If we view humans as socially conditioned, then the solution would have to be social change and behavioral reconditioning. If, however, we view humans as moral animals, as biological beings who have evolved the capacity for language and choice, then the transformation from violence to nonviolence can be accomplished through insight, personal responsibility, and choice.

The next chapter is a meditation on human nature. It is somewhat daunting to grapple with such a profound subject upon which no one has yet agreed. It is, perhaps, foolish to attempt it in one short chapter. Nevertheless, I will undertake it, cautiously and with a twofold purpose. First, I want to present a new paradigm of human nature which views motivation and choice from an evolutionary and, therefore, a biological perspective. This will show how human anger, aggression, and violence are rooted in human nature. We humans are biological creatures, similar to other animals in some ways, but radically different from all other animals in other ways. We are similar to other animals in that we are physical organisms who are energized by the life force. We are different from all other animals in that we have evolved the capacity for language. Language differentiates the human mind from the animal mind. It enables us to make choices and to construct a highly individuated sense of self. The sense of self, like the body, is energized by the life force but is different from the body in that this force manifests in language, choice, and social behavior.

The second purpose of the next chapter is to provide the interested reader with a conceptual model for understanding and transforming the energy of anger, aggression, and violence. This may be helpful to some. Others may prefer to get on with the job in which case, they may skip the next chapter and go directly to Step One. The view of human nature presented in the next chapter is integrated into all the Seven Steps like a foundation that one cannot see but that nevertheless holds up the house. If you are interested, come back to it later. It will help you to see yourself and the Seven Steps from a broader perspective.

2. On Human Nature

"To explain Adam's sin is therefore to explain original sin, and no explanation is of any avail which explains original sin and does not explain Adam. The deepest reason for this is to be discovered in the essential characteristic of human existence, that man is an individual and as such is at once himself and the whole race, in such wise that the whole race has part in the individual and the individual has part in the whole race . . . Adam is the first man; he is at once himself and the race . . . therefore what explains Adam explains the race and vice versa.

—Soren Kierkegaard, *The Concept of Dread*

If we want to understand the specific miseries that plague our own lives or the apparently inexplicable and unrelated horrors that roll off the daily press, we have to ask ourselves if there isn't something in each incident that is common to all—some deep, inherent tendency that, like a dark and ruinous river, runs through all of human existence. What does it mean to suggest that the root cause of all human anger, aggression, and violence lies in human nature? The answer lies in the idea of human nature itself.

What is "human" nature? The term is contradictory and confusing. When we think of nature we think of that which is not human, which is set off against the human, in contrast to it and "out there": the earth, the sky, animals, the growth and decay of organic matter, the rhythms and cycles of the seasons, the weather, the laws of physics to which humans must conform. When we think of the specifically human we think of something different, something apparently above and beyond the instinctual, reflexive, or determined processes of beasts and planets. We think of something that distinguishes the human from the merely brute, and it is that something which seems absolutely fundamental to our very humanness. We think of self-consciousness, personal identity and individual differences, of minds and souls, choices and consequences, of personalities and biographies, speech and writing, music, drama, and history, of love and hate, of compassion and murder, and war. The key to understanding human nature lies in this difference.

The idea of "human nature" connotes both the similarities and the differences between the animal and the human. Like it or not, we humans are animals, evolved from animals. Our bodies are in and of nature. Like animals, we are born, we grow old, and we die. Human physiology is not much different than the chimp's. Even the genomes of primates and humans vary only slightly. But humans are different than all other animals. Chimps can communicate but they cannot speak. They do not read and have no culture. In all the animal kingdom, the human is the only one with language. The human mind is sublime, "supernatural," beyond nature, set apart from it, if only as observer of it. At the same time the human mind is also in and of nature, having evolved from organismic life. The evolution of language has given us a unique capacity—the capacity to choose. Unlike animals, we can observe our minds, and we can change our minds.

Animals don't make choices in the way that humans do. Animals may make choices but they do not make *moral* choices. Animals seek pleasure and avoid pain. They choose what tastes good and feels good. Like young children, they are incapable of moral choice. If we are to transform the emotions that cause us suffering we need to be fully and clearly aware of the unique human capacity for choice. *If we want to shape ourselves where possible, if we want to guide our own development and maturation, then we must first affirm that by virtue of our fundamental nature we can.*

For three hundred years, since the rise of science, we have been debating whether human nature is basically shaped by nature or by nurture. Are we primarily animals governed by the laws of biology? Or are we empty slates at birth, shaped by culture, social conditions, and personal experience? Scientists say that we must be one or the other (or both) because only causal explanations are regarded as scientifically valid. To suggest that the fundamental basis of human nature rests upon the capacity for meaningful and moral choice is anathema to science. It is viewed as a throwback to pre-scientific times when our understanding of human nature came from holy texts, prophets, and philosophers.

The most extreme advocates of the view that humans are primarily animals are evolutionary biologists and biological psychiatrists. For social and political reasons which we shall not explore here, both are currently riding a crest of popularity. The term "biological psychiatry" contains a contradiction similar to that found in "human nature" in that "psyche" refers to mind or soul, and "biology" refers to the body. Biological psychiatry reduces the mind to the body. Biologists define an increasing variety of "normal" human behaviors as caused by genes and brain physiology. Biological psychiatrists define an increasing variety of "abnormal" (disturbing) human behavior as diseases caused by defective genes or errant brain chemistry. In both paradigms, nurture plays a minor role. Each argues that the primary causes of anger, aggression, and violence are physiologically determined.

The nurturalists believe that human nature is an unformed, pliable potentiality which is shaped by personal experience, family, culture, and society. They deny or minimize the influence of the body on human thought, emotions, and behavior. They believe that the causes of anger, aggression, and violence lie in other people and society. To the extent that they are bound to the models and methods of the physical sciences, psychological and sociological explanations are also causal-deterministic. The nurturalists leave out the body. The naturalists leave out the mind. Neither can provide a satisfactory place in their paradigms for choice.

On the other hand, if we view anger, aggression, and violence as governed by human will and choice, then the human situation can be improved by moral discourse, good will, conscious choice, and deliberate effort. If we dismiss the human capacity for choice as a delusion, or an incidental enigma too nebulous to consider, then our everyday language is a fraud, and we can only explain ourselves as automatons.

Humans are like animals in that we are *embodied.* We belong to the biological order of things, to the great chain of being. Of special interest here, and key to this model of human nature, is a particular characteristic that we share with all living beings. It is the precursor in the biological world to the human capacity for choice.

All living beings seek to sustain life (of the individual and/or the species) and to avoid death. This turning toward and turning away, toward life and away from death, is the most fundamental response to perceived phenomena in all of the biological order. I'll refer to it here as "bipolar reactivity."

Single-cell organisms, for example, are guided by tropisms. A tropism is a turning of all or part of an organism in response to an external stimulus. Paramecia are heliotropic. They turn towards the sun and away from darkness. Organisms turn towards pleasure and away from pain, towards safety and sustenance and away from danger and injury. These bipolar motivations are the instincts of survival, the basic intelligence of the life-force. Ponder this polarity. It energizes your body and your mind:

DESIRE   --   AVERSION
(I like it, want it)   --   (I don't like it, don't want it)

The basic, well-established premise of behavioral psychology is that all animals, including humans, are motivated by these bipolar desires. Rats, monkeys, and humans can all be trained to perform a particular action by reinforcing it with pleasure and to avoid a particular action by associating it with pain. Freud elegantly named this universal principle of bipolar reactivity "the pleasure principle." There is a significant difference, however, between the bipolar reactivity of animals and the bipolar reactivity of humans, one which corresponds to the difference between the animal and the human mind.

The key difference between the animal and the human mind—and the one upon which moral choice depends—is the human capacity for language, for speech and writing. The evolution of language created a new form of consciousness, a new realm of reality where symbols, ideas, and meanings are more important than physical things. Through language, objects acquire a symbolic existence separate from the physical object itself. The word "tree" signifies, but is different from the objective tree. Language can refer to something which exists but is not present—an absent beloved, our lost car keys. It can also refer to something which does not exist concretely—a horned rabbit, an ideal, a utopia, or a ghost.

Language gives us the capacity to name and, therefore, to make distinctions—me (not) you, us (not) them, near (not) far, up (not) down, in (not) out, etc. Linguistic consciousness is, itself, bipolar. It has also been called "dialectical" or "dualistic" consciousness. It operates by means of antithetical categories, such as "same" and "other," on which all classification systems are based. Every distinction is also an exclusion—"this/ not that."

The capacity to make distinctions enables the capacity for choice. If I can distinguish between "this" and "that" I can choose between them. The more distinctions I can make, the more choices I have.

As language and the capacity for choice evolved, the world became richer and more complex. The distinction between memory and anticipation, between past and future, gave rise to a sense of historical time. The awareness that some actions have desirable consequences and some have undesirable consequences gave rise to ethics. The capacity to name sharpened the awareness of self and other, generating a social consciousness. The antithetical concepts of self and other are the foundation of human society.

Personality theories are ideas about the nature and development of the self. The connection between language and the sense of self is revealed in the etymology of the word "personality." "Persona" is a Latin word which refers to the masks worn by characters in Roman plays, and has the meaning of both "mask" and "character." The Latin root of "persona" is *sonum*, which means "sound." The word "persona" originally meant "the sound coming through the mask." The persona of an actor in a play is created by the mask— or face—and speech, which displays his character. The etymology of "personality" reveals how the sense of self is based on language (including meaningful action) and relationship to others.

The consciousness of self and other creates a new form of relationship, not seen in the animal world, in which individuals relate to each other through language rather than through just the body. Our sense of ourselves and others is based not only on perceptions of the body, but also on the meanings which language gives to body, mind, and deed—strong or weak, smart or stupid, good or bad.

We humans, like animals, are not born with a *concept* of self. The concept of self grows in humans together with the development of language. Language is acquired and learned and is the prerequisite for everything that is distinctly human. The concept of self is an idea which is also acquired and learned.

As I have stated, animals and humans both desire physical pleasure, safety, and survival, and they both avoid physical pain, danger, and death. But the human linguistic mind also abstracts and sublimates these desires and fears and incorporates them into the sense of self. *The desire for pleasure is sublimated into the desire for happiness. The desire for life is sublimated into the desire to live forever. The fear of pain is sublimated into anxiety about future unhappiness. And the fear of death is sublimated into the fear of self-negation.* Human nature is thus characterized by both the biological polarity of physical desires and aversions and by the psychological polarity of self-interested desires and aversions. Understanding this is a key to transforming the energy of anger, aggression, and violence.

We can depict this idea simply in the diagram below where desire and aversion are integrated into a model of human nature which can accommodate both the reflexive responses of our biological nature and the abstracted, consciously motivated responses of our linguistic nature.

EGO

DESIRE   – ^ –   AVERSION

BODY

The sense of self is linked to the search for happiness and the avoidance of unhappiness. *In humans, the survival instinct is sublimated into striving for an enduring sense of self which is an object of value in a field of social meanings.* If we are to speak coherently about a solution to human aggression and violence we have to begin by clearly understanding its relationship to the universal desire for happiness.

The desire for happiness is a state of wanting what we do not or cannot have. It is a state of unhappy deprivation. If we were happy we would not seek happiness. The underbelly of the desire for happiness is dissatisfaction, frustration, and pain which kindle the fires of anger, aggression, and violence.

Everyone has their own formula for happiness, although we all toast to health, wealth, and long life. If you ask ordinary people what would make them happy they will tell you what they want and what they don't want. A student will say he will be happy if he gets good grades and graduates. He will be unhappy if he gets bad grades and is expelled. A businessman will say that he will be happy if he makes money and unhappy if he loses it. A person may be happy when he or she finds a mate and starts a family and unhappy until then. Someone else will be happy when he or she gets a new car, or has a sexual adventure, or goes on vacation. Many people would be happy if they could just have a cigarette, a drink, or some other fix.

People say they are happy when they have what they want and can avoid what they don't want. Conversely, they are unhappy when they don't get what they want or cannot escape the unwanted. Everyone has a "happiness project" in which they pursue what they think will make them happy in the future and avoid what they think will make them unhappy in the future. Our sense of self-worth is linked to the success of our happiness projects. If we think we will be happy in the future we will be happy today and feel good about ourselves. If we think we will be unhappy in the future we will be depressed today and feel badly about ourselves. A happy person has a high sense of self-esteem. An unhappy person feels worthless. People commit suicide when they are unhappy and cannot imagine being happy in the future. It is difficult to imagine a happy person with low self-esteem or an unhappy person with high self-esteem.

The problem is that our happiness projects are tragically flawed and this tragic flaw is also at the core of human nature. The Hellenic Greeks had a keen sense of tragedy as a darkness in human life, a sense that all happiness projects are fated eventually to fail or fade, finally at death. Freud thought that humans are not meant to be happy. "Everything is against it," he said. Freud identified three main causes of human unhappiness: the body, nature, and relationships. The body causes unhappiness because it is impermanent and is doomed to sickness, suffering, and death. Nature causes unhappiness because it is indifferent to our desires and periodically inflicts destruction upon us. Relationships cause unhappiness because our desires conflict and we all want our own way.

Our happiness projects are flawed because our desires and fears are endless and because they conflict. Sometimes they are in conflict with the desires and fears of others and may spawn violence, murder, and war. Sometimes our own desires and fears conflict—the essence of neurotic conflict. As long as we live there is always more to be desired, more to be grasped and eaten, more life to be lived, more self-enhancement to be won. There is no end to it, no final paradise on Earth where all desires are gratified and all the unwanted avoided. The source of our unhappiness is that we can't have everything we want, we cannot avoid some things we don't want, and our fragile, self-constructed sense of self is vulnerable to negation, disappointment, and death.

The fear of death is endless until it is ended by death itself. Death finally dooms all of our happiness projects and obliterates the sense of self, unless we have (or think we have) discovered the key to immortality.

I once asked a Tibetan lama to define "neurosis," a term his translator used often to refer to psychological suffering. He said, "Neurosis is a complex of desires, aversions, and suffering." He had no psychoanalytic training, but I'm sure Freud would have agreed with his definition. Our desires and our fears are woven into a tangled web of conflicts. Sometimes we want both to eat dessert and to be thin. Or we want money but don't want to work. Or we want to be married and also to be free of obligations. *Whatever we think will make us happy is what we will suffer from.* All of the painful emotions are generated by failed happiness projects.

The human sense of self is extremely delicate and vulnerable to the vicissitudes of life. A serious threat to our happiness projects is a threat to our sense of self and can be experienced as a threat to life itself. Animals react to danger to life and limb with the fight-flight reaction. They fight or run to overcome or escape the danger. Humans react the same way in the defense of self. *Human anger, aggression, and violence are fight responses to a perceived threat to the sense of self and its happiness projects.*

Transforming the energy of anger requires deeply investigating our basic nature and becoming familiar with it. The Oracle of Delphi advised the Greeks: "know thyself." In this sense, knowledge is truly power. With self-knowledge comes the power to master oneself, to heal oneself, and to transform the energy of anger, aggression, and violence.

Transforming yourself means relating to yourself and to life differently. It is a radical program. It means understanding that your mind gives you the capacity to make meaningful and discriminating choices, and that what you do matters. It means becoming a more mature person. The ideal of maturity is expressed in a version of the Serenity Prayer: the courage, tempered by moderation and compassion, to do what one wants and avoid what one doesn't want; the serenity to accept not getting what one wants and getting what one doesn't want; and the wisdom to know the difference and to act responsibly. It means understanding both your power and your powerlessness. A good definition of maturity is "the willingness to give things up, to let go." Children demand. The wise let go. The wise focus on their input into life rather than on outcomes. *The secret to the transformation of the energy of anger is to let go of what you want, if relentlessly pursuing it would lead to suffering for yourself or others, and to open to the unwanted which you cannot avoid no matter how painful it may be.*

Following is a seven-step guide to understanding and transforming the energy of anger. To succeed, you must have the courage and stamina to face yourself and the unshakable commitment to heal yourself. If this seven-step program is undertaken with patience, effort, and perseverance it will bear fruit. If it is undertaken lightly, halfheartedly, or with the expectation of quick results it is guaranteed to fail.

3. Step One: Becoming Aware I

Developing Awareness

THE FIRST STEP on the path to understanding and healing anger, aggression, and violence is to develop an awareness of them. I don't mean an intellectual awareness, or a fleeting recall of having been angry in the past and a quick mental acknowledgment of it. I mean turning your attention inward to your mind and becoming familiar with the landscape and sea swells of anger, aggression, and violence in all their textures, contours, and subtleties.

Anger is a normal human emotion. Everyone experiences the feeling of anger. An emotion, as the name implies, is an energy that moves us. It generates energy and action. Anger is an emotion which manifests as an inner experience, as a complex of bodily feelings, and as thought, speech, and action.

Anger can lead to aggression and violence. The word "aggression" is derived from the Latin *aggredi,* meaning "to attack." Not all aggression is fueled by anger. A chess player can aggressively attack his game without anger. A football player or a boxer can be aggressive without being angry. When anger fuels aggression, however, it can become destructively violent.

Since anger is an emotion, the first step on the path to understanding and healing anger, aggression, and violence is to turn your attention inward. Anger breeds in the mind. If we are to become familiar with its fluctuating energy, we must first be willing to cultivate a deep and direct intimacy with our own minds. If we are to learn to ride its energies we must make friends with it, just as a trainer must make friends with a horse he is trying to tame.

Most of the time our attention is focused outwards: on other people, on things, on the course of events. We are interested in how things are going. Are they going our way? Will our car start in the morning? Will our boss like us or are we in danger of being fired? Is our family safe and healthy? Are we going to get what we want and avoid what we don't want? Will our plans for future happiness be realized or frustrated?

When we are angry, we usually blame outer events. Someone didn't act right. Things didn't go right. But if anger breeds in the mind, if it is a *reaction* to people and events, then we have the power to skillfully ride its energies. Other people or external events may provoke us, but they don't cause our anger. Remember this vital lesson: Your anger arises in your mind. You can know it only by turning inward to your mind. You can tame it only by training your mind. This means that you have the option of processing the provocation, reflecting upon it, evaluating it, and *choosing* a response. Your mind is intermediate between the provocative external events and your body–your speech and action. A man may pull a gun on you but you have the option of fighting him, running, or raising your hands. Your wife may yell at you but you have the choice of whether to listen, to defend yourself, or to retaliate. Remember, the essence of your humanity is your capacity to choose.

We all want to make intelligent choices, the right choices. To make intelligent choices we must understand how our minds work. Fortunately, we don't have to reinvent the wheel. From the dawn of human self-awareness, people have been searching within themselves, seeking insight and mastery. Over time, many methods for developing awareness have evolved. In modern America, psychotherapy is the most popular approach to examining and analyzing the mind, and when people have mental or emotional problems, they usually consult a psychotherapist for help.

People come to psychotherapy because they are unhappy. They are suffering mentally or emotionally. Most of the time, they don't have a clear idea of why they are suffering or unhappy, and they don't know what to do about it. Therapy can help by inquiring into the nature of their suffering, by relating it to the problems of their lives, and by exploring possible choices that might relieve it. A skillful therapist is a guide who encourages insight and constructive action. In this sense, therapy is an educational undertaking. The client is the agent of change. In my forty years of practicing psychotherapy I have never changed anyone. I have never "excised" anyone's anger. But many people have changed of their own accord and by their own power of choice.

Unfortunately, psychotherapy has come under the dominating influence of medical psychiatry. Many psychotherapists, both medical and non-medical, think that their task is to diagnose and "treat" their patients rather than to help them understand the workings of their minds and to help them heal themselves. Under the influence of the medical model, a tragically misguided movement is afoot to view the psychotherapist in the same terms as a medical physician, and to evaluate psychotherapy according to "objective" criteria which mimic the quantitative measurements appropriate to the physical sciences. Psychotherapy is different than medicine.

A skillful medical doctor may or may not be able to heal the patient, but she practices her art upon a relatively passive subject. No surgeon asks his patient to understand the intricacies of the human body and help guide the knife. The patient has only to follow the physician's instructions. In psychotherapy, much also depends on the skill of the therapist. But the outcome of psychotherapy turns upon the motivations and capacity of the client. I have written extensively about the medical model and its social functions and limitations. Suffice it to say here, I believe that the medical model is a metaphor which views the mind as if it is a physical organ and, thus, interferes with understanding and with helping the client to heal as a human person.

If we drop the medical model, we see that people come to therapy with problems that can best be understood as existential dilemmas. They don't bring us diseases, they bring us life problems. They may have been influenced by psychiatric ideology and media publicity and wonder out loud about their psychiatric diagnosis and their brain chemistry. But in the end, they don't really care about diagnosis except, possibly, for insurance reimbursement. They want to feel better and to enjoy life. The word "patient" comes from the Greek *pathos*, which means "suffering." The words pathology, pity, patience, and patient are derivatives and connote the concept of suffering at their core. Whether we call them patients or clients, those who come to us for help are sufferers. Everyone suffers, including therapists. We are all "patients" who suffer from the trials of life and death and seek relief.

My approach to psychotherapy evolved when I rejected the medical model as the most effective paradigm for understanding human psychic suffering, and turned my attention to the vast and startlingly precise exegesis on human psychology in the Buddhist wisdom tradition. The Seven Steps outlined in this book are a synthesis of Western psychology and Buddhist psychology.

A basic Buddhist teaching is "the four thoughts that turn the mind inward." In ordinary language, these thoughts teach that happiness is not to be found in the external world, nor is unhappiness. Happiness and unhappiness are properties of mind. We naturally want to be happy forever, but our experience is marked by suffering, impermanence, and the lack of enduring substance in anything. We want to hold on to the people and situations we love, but everything changes. Everything appears and disappears. Our body is precious to us but is destined to die. In this predicament, what we do is important. How we manage and conduct ourselves makes a difference to our happiness and the happiness of others.

The same insight is expressed in the Hindu concept of *kundalini tantra*. In this tradition, the life force is metaphorically depicted as a serpent seated at the base of the spinal cord. The subtle body, i.e., the mind, has seven ascending nodes, or *chakras,* representing stages in the evolution of consciousness. The three lower chakras, below the diaphragm, are the seat of the base, animal functions of the body—the desires for food, sex, and power. To transform the suffering caused by the energy of the lower chakras, kundalini practice raises this energy to the higher centers—the compassionate heart, intelligent speech, wisdom, and joy. The raising of the kundalini energy is a metaphor for the deliberate transformation of self from the base to the subtle, from suffering to happiness. The kundalini is a metaphor but one that, unlike the determinism of the medical model, guides the conscious efforts of the sufferer to evolve a "higher" state of consciousness.

Not surprisingly, the same idea is expressed in Christian thought. The Christian Gospel represents an evolution of consciousness beyond outward conformity to the Mosaic teachings on law and conduct to a concern with the inner, spiritual dimensions of life. I once asked my teacher, Khenpo Karthar Rinpoche, to define the word "spiritual." His answer was striking: "Anything pertaining to mind." The teachings of Jesus provide a solution to the problem of human suffering and violence which go beyond the external regulation of conduct to a willed transformation of the inner self.

As Christianity evolved, the complexity of the human sense of self also evolved and the problem of the relief of suffering was formulated in the metaphors of an interior transformation. St. Augustine (354–430 C.E.) taught that the spiritual path is a journey from the earthly city of humanity to the heavenly City of God—from the desire for sensuous pleasure, to rational understanding, to wisdom, grace, and happiness.

In Western non-Christian thought, the same idea is expressed by the Stoics, among many others. Epictetus (c.55 – c.135 C.E.), who was probably influenced by Buddhist thought coming down the Silk Road from India to Greece, said: "What disturbs people's minds is not events but their judgments on events." Good and evil, suffering and happiness, he taught, are the consequence of human choice. In this tradition, the path to happiness lies in the development of awareness, reason, and the capacity for rational choice.

The same idea is the basis of modern cognitive psychotherapy. Albert Ellis, the founder of rational-emotive behavioral therapy (REBT) teaches the "ABCs of anger." The basic principle of REBT is that our anger is not caused by Activating external events (A), although they are certainly factors. It is caused by Irrational Beliefs (B) which lead us to a Consequent (C) rejection of life as it is and other people as they are, and the painful emotions which stem from such rejection. An unrealistic view of the world leads to erroneous judgments and errant actions, which cause pain to ourselves and others. We become angry at others not because of how they behave but because of how we evaluate their behavior in relation to our own interests. Our beliefs, judgments, and choices are products of our minds. Our interests and desires are products of our minds and bodies. Mind is the mediator between the activating event and the consequent outburst of anger.

"Psychotherapy" means, literally, ministering to the mind (or psyche). Experienced and skillful psychotherapists adopt various techniques for developing insight. When I was a resident in psychiatry I learned an important technique which I use often. One of my teachers advised: "When the patient talks about feelings, ask her about the thoughts that accompany those feelings. When he expresses an idea or tells a story, ask him what feelings arise as he thinks about it." Human language, thought, desires, and aversions are woven into a single fabric. An experienced therapist knows what questions to ask to lead the patient to an awareness of mind and feelings. If the therapist knows how to work with her own mind, she can help the patient to work with his.

When I meet a new patient for the first time, I ask myself: What is the nature of his suffering? What negative emotion is he suffering from? Is anxious? Depressed? Angry? During this first interview I watch the patient carefully, looking for clues. Therapy begins with and depends upon the therapist's awareness of the patient. Without it, the therapist cannot help the patient to become aware of him or herself. What does his facial expression say? Is her forehead tensely wrinkled and her mouth in a sad droop or an angry grimace? Is his body tense or relaxed? Does he seem confident or confused? Does she keep a personal distance as if she is afraid of me? Is he trying to impress or convince me? Or does she treat me as a friend whom she hopes can help her? It often happens that a patient looks angry but doesn't speak angrily or want to admit to being angry. In such a situation, I might say: "You looked to me to be angry in the waiting room. Are you?" The response is usually a jolt of awareness, an initial denial, and, usually, an eventual admission of anger that brings a sense of clarity and relief.

As we become aware of the working of our mind, we'll find ourselves grappling with an inner trickster. Pay attention! The mind in which anger arises is also the mind that holds it, hides it, fans it, justifies it, or suppresses it. That's why the first step is crucial—before we can understand, befriend, tame, and transform our anger, we have to recognize it clearly and acknowledge it frankly. This is no small task.

Whether we seek the help of a therapist or launch out on our own, self-awareness is a precondition for understanding and healing our anger. If we become aware of the workings of our mind we can discover the means by which we create our anger and the key to healing it. If we become aware that we are harboring irrational beliefs, ideas with false premises, mistaken assumptions or flawed logic, we can examine them and correct them. If we discover that we cherish ideas which are not in harmony with the realities of life and nature we can learn to relax into existence. If we find that we harbor desires, hopes, and expectations which cannot be achieved we have the option of letting them go.

Psychotherapists and their patients/clients can benefit from the wisdom of many traditions, practices, philosophies, and teachings that lie outside the domain of traditional Western psychology. To develop awareness is to take a journey within—into the heart of our being. It is the mythic journey in which the hero, striving for a noble goal, ventures bravely into the unknown, facing the darkest terrors and the most fearsome obstacles. The path to self-knowledge leads through the dark night of the soul. As my first teacher, Agehananda Bharati, warned me when I told him I was going to search for a Buddhist teacher: "It is not a path for the fainthearted."

Our attention is ordinarily focused outside ourselves, on other people and events. In the first session, I ask my patients: "What's the problem? What are you unhappy about? What is your pain?" I ask them to tell me the story of their lives. They talk about their parents, their wives and children, their lovers, their work. The problem is outside themselves–in their relationships, their jobs, or their finances. Or they are unhappy with themselves. When they do turn inward, they feel badly about themselves. They blame themselves. Often they complain of painful feelings. They are anxious but don't know why. Or they are angry and feel justified but don't know what to do about it. Or they are depressed and often, in these days of the medicalization of the mind, they think they have a chemical imbalance, or a vague mental "disease" over which they have no control.

At the same time that our attention is normally focused outside of ourselves, or on our confused self-narratives, there is a strong, restless undercurrent of mental activity constantly flowing just beneath our awareness like water flowing under ice. I call this stream of activity "hypermentation" because it is excessive, unnecessary, and provokes painful feelings. There is nothing wrong with mentation–thinking. We think to solve problems. Reasoning is thinking. Knowing is thinking. Science and logic require thinking. Thinking can be enjoyable, a scintillating collage of satisfying conversations with one's self–words, phrases, images, stories we tell about ourselves and others, memories and reminiscences, hopes and plans, fantasies and daydreams, all fiction—all fabricated by the creative imagination. Thinking can also go wild. It can go into an incessant, uninterruptible torrent of words and images, frustrated desires, and implacable worries that turn life into a nightmare.

William James had an interesting idea about human mentation, particularly human intelligence. Influenced by Darwin, he believed that the human mind evolved as a problem solver in the service of the survival of the individual and the species. This makes sense. Survival requires solving the problems of existence. The human mind is the most evolved instrument of species survival (and, when it goes wrong, of species extinction). Modern progress is the fruit of science, which is, basically, a method for solving problems through careful observation and reasoning. Biologically speaking, the human mind is a problem seeker, a problem finder, and a problem solver. People love puzzles. Buddha had the same idea. He taught his disciples: "Your ego is the sum of your problems." No problems, no ego needed. The function of the ego is to scan the life field for problems, for threats to its happiness projects.

Hypermentation is thinking gone haywire. It is the apparently autonomous activity of the undisciplined, problem-solving mind which obsessively and incessantly surveys the life field looking for satisfaction and trouble. Busy mind is like a police scanner going from station to station until it finds something interesting, or a problem. Daydreams, fantasies, and creative imagination can be pleasant, but they distract from life in the present moment. They are wish fulfillments, motivated by the desire for pleasure and happiness. The other side of the coin of hypermentation is worry–the fear that things will go wrong. The ego has no problem finding problems. There are many more ways for things to go wrong than for them to go right. The hypermentating mind will make problems if it can't find any, and react emotionally with anxiety, anger, or depression as if they are actually happening. Much of our mental suffering is due to undisciplined, hardly noticed thinking about the actual or potential problems of life. As Mark Twain said: "No one knows the troubles I've seen—most of which never happened."

Unattended, this flickering stream of thoughts, images, and feelings goes on by itself, carrying us this way and that, without our understanding that much of the story of our lives is being written in the dark. Most of us are usually more or less "on automatic." We rarely direct our attention to our own minds. We are more often self-conscious than self-aware. What we ordinarily call self-consciousness is usually an exaggerated state of self-reference in relation to others. The self-conscious person is thinking about what others are thinking of him or her. It is an anxious sense of self that makes us stumble.

One of my patients, an adolescent boy, was so focused on how (he thought) others saw him that when he walked into the school cafeteria he lost his natural walking rhythm, which increased his self-conscious anxiety that others would see him "walking funny." He was caught in a trap of his own making. Had he been self-aware, he might have recognized his desire to be liked and his fear of humiliation and worked with it in his own mind rather than projecting onto others and, both literally and figuratively, losing his sense of balance. It is important to distinguish between the awareness that allows us to see and work with our emotions and the self-consciousness that is merely a function of worried and confused hypermentation.

I often encounter people in and out of my office who seem to be lost in thought. I sometimes ask them what they are thinking about. They are usually startled by the question. They look at me blankly and are often surprised to hear themselves admit with embarrassment that they don't know or can't say. Or they describe one small, fleeting fragment of disconnected thought. The "normal" human state of mind is constant, incessant thinking—an enigmatically linked stream of consciousness, sensations, memories, feelings, desires, fears, and chatter. And at the center of the narrative, the star of the show is always—ME! This is why the first leg of the journey requires courage. To become familiar with the chaotic, egotistical, and often nonsensical narrative of our own mind stream is disconcerting and painful. To discover directly that we are literally "lost in thought" can be frightening. But this is where we are and where we must begin.

It's consoling to remember that everyone is neurotic, each one of us. The "normal" mind suffers from a complex of conflicting desires and aversions. The best we can do is to become aware of our neuroses, to become wiser in our thinking and our conduct of life. In my experience, meditation is the most direct and efficient method for developing self-awareness. Self-awareness is not a steady state because experience is not a steady state. Through the practice of meditation, we can learn to watch our ever-fluctuating mental processes from a more detached, aerial perspective. Without necessarily understanding ourselves in some intellectual way, we can directly discover how the mind works. The mind has its causes and effects, its motivations and intentions, and its awareness and evaluation of their possible consequences.

The often-misunderstood idea of *karma* refers to our motivations and intentions and their consequences. Many people think it means something like "fate" or "destiny." Indeed it does, but this is only half its meaning. The word "karma" comes from a Sanskrit word which means "action." Specifically, it means "intended action." Moreover, it means "intended action and its consequences." As we develop awareness of our desires, our aversions, and our intentions, we also develop the ability to distinguish the consequences that flow from them.

Buddhist philosophy defines karma as the ineluctable moral law of cause and effect. We find some variation of that principle in every wisdom tradition. It expresses an ancient insight that good actions lead to good consequences and bad actions lead to bad consequences. Leaving aside for the moment what is a good or bad action, or what is a good or bad consequence, the principle of karma is that our intentions and actions have consequences which shape our future experiences. This is the meaning of the ancient Greek axiom "character is fate." Our character is shaped by what we do, by how we relate to our desires, our aversions, and our self-interest. What we do counts. How we think and act will shape our lives and our future happiness, as well as the lives and happiness of others.

I was once asked how my practice of meditation helps my practice of psychotherapy. I said that it helps me to understand myself and the workings of mind so I can better help others to help themselves. I don't force meditation on anyone, or even suggest it. People can be taught how to quiet their mind and body without calling it "meditation." Although some forms of meditation are practiced in the context of religious belief, the method presented here does not advocate or promote any particular religion. It is simply a method for developing and practicing awareness.

Many psychotherapists are meditators. They have joined meditation groups or gone on retreats to learn how to practice. I offer free meditation sessions in my office on Friday evenings entirely separate from my therapy practice. My patients are free to attend or not. It doesn't make any difference what the tradition or lineage of the teacher is. You don't have to accept any religion or doctrine, or study theology, to develop awareness. To work with your anger, there is nothing better than to sit and directly observe the workings of your mind.

The term "meditation" carries with it a burden of trendy, pseudo-mystical connotations. The biggest mistake people make is to think that they will "get something" out of meditation. It would be more accurate to think they will be getting rid of something. Awareness practice undermines our unwitting subjugation to hypermentation. It cuts through the cascade of thoughts and feelings that distract us from the present moment where life actually happens. The inner newsreel, with its imagined or distorted dramas, becomes less urgent and seductive. The unexamined hopes and fears that have thrown us into automatic or reflexive behavior lose their power to toss us about. What we get rid of, initially, is a great deal of compelling noise with no point or real substance to it. Even by becoming aware of its nature we de-reify it, render it less solid and intractable.

Hindus call this discursive chatter "the veil of *maya*"—the fictional, illusory thoughts which cloud our perception of things as they are. The Bible calls it "seeing as through a glass darkly." The first fruit of basic meditation is a quieter mind. In the Tibetan tradition, the beginner's basic meditation is called *shamatha*, which is often translated as "dwelling in peace." It is also sometimes called "calm abiding" or "tranquilizing meditation." The "tranquility" of tranquilizing meditation is the antithesis of the fuzzy, mind-numbing tranquility of tranquilizing drugs. It is a state of calm clarity.

How can we sort out our neuroses when the mind is a wild, chaotic mess of fragmented thought? How can we work with our anger when we experience it as a deluge of highly charged, urgent impulses, all mixed in with fleeting bits of narrative, physical sensations, whispers of memory, rushes of fear, and the visceral press to act? We can't. Every beginning meditator discovers very quickly that the mind has a mind of its own. No beginner sits down, says, "Peace! Be still!" and accomplishes enlightenment. It's enough at the start just to see, discover, and acknowledge the chatter. That, in itself, is a great step towards self-awareness. Chogyam Trungpa Rinpoche taught that the awareness of our confusion is the first step towards clarity.

Over time, we can learn to just take note of whatever arises without being pushed and pulled emotionally. We can sit still and not respond reflexively to our hypermentation. We can allow ourselves to rest, to gently release thoughts, to find a quiet space apart from the discursive jumble. We can choose to be simply and quietly aware. In these quiet moments, experiences arise much more clearly and distinctly. Only then can we discover the source of our suffering and our anger.

I once attended a conference between a highly esteemed Tibetan lama, Jamgon Kongtrul Rinpoche, and a group of psychiatrists. Someone asked Rinpoche: "What is meditation?" Rinpoche looked playfully puzzled, pretended not to understand, and after a brief consultation with his translator, answered: "Meditation? Meditation? I don't know what that means. We have another word for it which means 'paying attention to.'" Whatever the style, to meditate is to pay attention.

In traditional sitting meditation, paying proper attention to the mind requires that the body be in the proper attentive position. The traditional lotus or cross-legged sitting posture is best for focusing attention on the mind, but you can also sit with your legs loosely crossed, or you can sit in a comfortable chair. The act of attention requires the posture of attention. The posture must be neither too tense nor too relaxed, for these extremes mirror the mental extremes of agitation and laxity. By paying attention to the agitation or laxity of the mind we can find the balance of relaxed attention between these two extremes. The art of attention is a balancing of body and mind between effort and relaxation.

It helps to find a quiet place to sit in order to pay attention to the constant stream of mental activity. At the beginning, this may mean a quiet, external setting where one can sit without distractions. In my experience, I can see the workings of my mind more clearly if I sit outdoors, by a still pond, or in a silent wood. But the quiet one seeks is within. Krishnamurti used to ask, "Who is at peace? The person who sits in a quiet forest with a busy mind or the person who walks in a busy marketplace with a quiet mind?"

Begin by paying attention to your body and settling into it. The mind sits in the body like a lady in a buggy and if the buggy shakes, the lady shakes. This takes time and patience. Some people are naturally well-seated in their bodies. They tend to be athletes and, in this sense, meditation is an athletic event. Others are not comfortable in their bodies and must persevere with patience to find their seat. Learning to quiet the body is crucial for taming anger because anger carries such a strongly excited physiology. Calming the body in meditation is training for calming the body as anger rises. Just to be physically still when slight physical discomfort or restless mentation urges action undermines the blind and automatic reflexivity that binds us in destructive habits. Can you quietly sit for sixty seconds with an itchy nose? Invariably, the intensity of the itch rises, peaks, and subsides. So it is with anger. See for yourself.

We are distracted from the present moment where life happens by the incessant stream of discursive thought—remembering things past, ruminating about present problems, imagining future successes and failures. If you watch closely, you will see a gap between the thoughts. The quiet space is this gap, as when we turn the TV off and the room falls silent. The more we are able to rest in that gap of quiet awareness without discursive thought, the more our level of awareness will sharpen. With practice, the chatter will gradually settle down and the gaps will widen. By relaxing into the gaps, we calm the mind.

This is not an easy task. You have to train your mind. It is like training a puppy. Tell a puppy to sit and it may sit for a second then jump up happily wagging its tail. Tell it to sit again, and again and again, and it will gradually learn to sit until you tell it to come. Meditation practice is like that. It requires effort, perseverance, and patience—virtues which are very handy in everyday life.

One of the first things we discover during meditation is how difficult it is to disengage from our hypermentations. Discursive thought is the narrative of our identity and our lives. The mind is constantly searching for the answer to fundamental questions: "Who am I?" "What is the meaning of life?" "What shall I do?" We feel it is vital to keep thinking so we can figure things out. Dropping discursive thought is like dropping out of our autobiographies–our life stories. Then who are we? Nobody! What are we to do? Nobody going nowhere! Dropping discursive thought is like letting our guard down. We become anxious about our uncertainty, bewilderment, and disorientation. We could feel as if we are dying. Our reluctance to drop discursive thought, to let go of ourselves, reveals to us how tightly we hold on to our habitual sense of ourselves.

Once we learn to relax into the gap between thoughts the mind gradually opens into a clear, peaceful place of refuge from which we can gaze upon our mind stream with equanimity. It is as if we are sitting off to the side watching our neurotic narrative and behavior. This refuge is within ourselves, every one of us. If we seek, it can be found. It is our birthright, our nature. People from different cultures and religions have discovered it. Christian mystics sometimes call it "the witness" or "resting in the presence." Psychoanalysts call it "the observing self." Buddhists call it "the watcher." Developing awareness means identifying with the quiet observer rather than with the narrative. It is simply a change in perspective. One does not necessarily have to change anything else in life. But one will begin to see life in a different way.

The first level of awareness from the quiet place is mindfulness of the body and the senses—sight, sound, smell, taste, touch, and body position and movement. It is a kind of awakening to ourselves and the world around us. We become aware of our body sitting on a cushion or chair. We have the simple sense of our head, neck, and torso resting on the triangular foundation of crossed legs. Is your head centered on your neck? Is your spine arched in plumb with gravity? Do your legs ache?

The painfulness of sitting at attention makes us aware of the second level of mindfulness, our feelings of liking some states of mind and disliking others. We don't like it when our legs ache. We don't want to be in pain. We want to feel good and enjoy ourselves. We judge every experience: "I like it," "I don't like it," or "neutral." By noting these feelings, we become aware of the basic operations of mind: the desire for pleasure and the aversion to pain. We must learn not to judge our mind stream, to be tolerant of it. This is simply how the mind works. Thoughts and feelings arise, they peak, and they decay, leading to a new cycle of birth, life, and death.

As we develop the first two levels of awareness we can turn our quiet attention to the inner, discursive narratives we create about ourselves and our lives. The narrative is not a physical form. But our feelings of liking, disliking, or indifference are projected onto both form and narrative. We have physical desires and aversions. We may like ice cream and hate spinach. We may prefer to be warm rather than cold. We also have desires and fears about ourselves and our lives. We have plans and hopes for the future and we worry anxiously that things may go wrong. We want to be happy and fear that we will be unhappy. We want what we want. And we want to avoid anything that interferes with our happiness projects. In meditation, we begin to see—and to see through—the stories that we tell ourselves. We see the panic and confusion that arise whenever we are in danger of not getting what we want or of getting what we don't want.

Developing awareness of anger thus involves a sequence of steps taken, at first, one at a time and, gradually, all together. It requires first developing the intention, the effort, and the perseverance to calm your mind by means of some kind of mind-stabilizing practice. There are numerous methods to cultivate meditative awareness besides the one briefly described here, such as yoga and martial arts. Whatever practice you choose, you must develop the skill to pay attention to the present moment if you are to catch anger as it arises which is, by far, the best time to catch it. As you develop awareness you will be amazed to see more clearly the many faces of anger.

4. Step One: Becoming Aware II

THE MANY FACES OF ANGER

TO UNDERSTAND and heal anger we must become aware of it as it arises and pervades the mind—easy to say, but not so easy to do. We are overcome and distracted by our intense feelings. We are blinded by our habitual patterns of thinking about anger and may not recognize it, even as we feel it. We tend to stereotype anger as hot, overt aggression. We picture a menacing, beet-faced man lost in his rage, ranting and raving epithets, threatening violence, destruction, or revenge. Hot, overt anger is obvious to the angry person as well as to those around him. But overt anger is just the tip of the iceberg. Anger has many faces. It is a chameleon, a master of disguise. Its patterns, textures, and coloration change from context to context. To become aware of our anger we must become aware of its many faces.

People reveal their anger differently—through their bodily kinesics, their facial expression, their words and tone of voice, or their actions. Paradoxically, anger can manifest in thought without apparent affect. One can think coldly of revenge against an enemy without feeling the heat of the anger. Or, it can manifest in affect without conscious thought content as a chaotic feeling of general frustration and irritability with no idea, or only a dim, partially repressed idea of what it is, what has caused it, or towards whom it is directed.

Although anger can generate aggression and violence, it is possible to feel angry without being aggressive and to be aggressive without feeling anger. Everyone sometimes becomes angry with their children, spouse, parents, or friends without being aggressive towards them. Sometimes we think we are getting angry at people we love for their sake, although our true motivation may be selfish. When anger is motivated by aversion or hatred, it can become aggressive and destructive. But when anger is motivated by love or compassion it can be constructive. Nonviolent anger at apartheid, racism, discrimination, exploitation, abusiveness, bullying, or injustice of any kind may help to generate positive social change

———————

Anger can be hot or cold, personal or impersonal, overt or disguised. Sometimes our anger is expressed blatantly in words and deeds— through rudeness, insults, slander, or physical violence. Sometimes it is weak and fleeting, a flutter of energy which quickly subsides. Sometimes our anger is cold and enduring. We may act it out passively through hurtful inaction by ignoring, snubbing, or subtly sabotaging the person we blame. Anger can manifest in assault and murder but it can also be subtle, a barely perceptible coldness of tone, a stiff handshake, or a tense smile. It can hide itself in excuses and self-justifications, in rationalizations and denial, in tightness, indifference, or rejection. It can find expression in violent revenge or in the slightest withdrawal of warmth, a stony silence, or avoidance.

Where people are bound together by attachment and guilt, and the relationship seems secure, they may feel freer to express their anger in physical or verbal violence or in subtle oppositional defiance, defensiveness, or neglect. In families, anger often finds expression as sugarcoated criticism, competitiveness, rudeness, harshness, or sarcasm. It can mask itself in baiting or biting words, in cutting humor, in teasing and kidding around. Sometimes the husband or wife may withhold sex, neglect chores, or be emotionally cool and distant as a subtle expression of resentment. Often, the angry person does not recognize the feeling of anger, or may name it differently or deny it altogether.

The resistance to recognizing anger is a fatal impediment to developing awareness of it and skillfully riding its energies. Some people only become aware of their anger with the help of someone else—a friend, a lover, a priest, or a psychotherapist who confronts them. Sometimes, we have to be confronted repeatedly and painfully before we are willing to admit it and look at its effects on our lives and the lives of others. The main resistance to the awareness of anger is pride. If we are too proud to consider the possibility that our passive resistance, our polite tightness, our moping depression, or our cool tenseness is anger, there is no possibility of transforming it. Unless we become aware of our anger, experience it, reflect on it, and accept it for what it is, we will not be able to understand, tame, or heal it.

The sheer energy of its most authentic manifestation as overt, hot anger is so volcanic, so overwhelming, that it can only come from the life force itself, in defense of itself. This is a vital insight into why taming anger seems to be such a Herculean task. It is the life force defending itself which must be tamed. The name of one of the monasteries where I studied is Namgyal. *Gyal* means "conqueror" in Tibetan. *Nam* is an intensifier. "Namgyal" is an honorific name meaning "extreme conqueror." The conquest, however, is not over anyone or anything else. It is a conquest of one's self, of one's negative energies, attitudes, and emotions.

Anger is fueled by the energy of our basic emotions, by our frustrated desires and aversions struggling against obstacles and inevitabilities, striving for satisfaction and control. Sometimes our frustrations are immediate and obvious. We miss the bus that connects to the only train that can get us to our urgent appointment on time. A stranger accidentally backs into our new car. At other times, our frustrations are vague and unidentifiable. We are irritable and faintly angry at little things with an inchoate presentiment that something more significant is bothering us, but we can't get clear on what it is.

Often, we are not clear about our anger because we are not clear about our motivations, about what we want and don't want. Some of the most vital human desires are sublime and subtle. The words "sublime" and "subtle" are related to "sublimate" and "subliminal." When dry ice evaporates it sublimates from a solid to a gas. The solid ice is like the body, tangible and visible. The carbon dioxide gas is like the mind, invisible, intangible, beyond the limits of direct perception. When gobbling food is sublimated into epicurean dining the gluttony is sublimated and imperceptible. When sex is loving, lust is sublimated into affection. Ego desires are not physical or tangible. They are abstract, often beyond the limits of our perception, so that we are unaware of what we want and what we don't want.

Among the desires of which we are often unaware are the desires to create a stable, solid sense of self, to feel good about ourselves, and to be in control of our lives. When these desires are frustrated they can become the breeding ground of our anger. Anything which threatens or negates our sense of self, which makes us feel bad, or anxious, or helpless, or interferes with our happiness projects may unleash the energy of anger, aggression, and violence. The idea that our happiness project itself, our striving for happiness, is the source of our suffering is a confusing paradox and a bitter pill to swallow. This is why courage, honesty, and a self-reflective awareness are necessary conditions for understanding and healing anger, aggression, and violence.

In family therapy and other social situations one can often recognize angry people and at whom they are angry by their tone of voice and body kinesics. John and Alice brought their son, Adam, for a consultation because of his behavior problems at home. They presented Adam as the patient, but I focused on the family system. When Alice spoke to her son her voice was warm and tender. When she addressed her husband it had a touch of coolness and reserve. I mentioned the difference in her tone of voice and asked her if she was angry with her husband. At first, she denied it. But John interrupted and referred to several recent instances of her being angry with him at home.

They often argued over how to set limits and discipline for their son. John was more strict and thought Alice indulged Adam too much and too often. He also complained about her disinterest in sex. Alice explained her disinterest in sex as a premenopausal symptom, but she admitted to the disagreements about parenting Adam. As she expressed her feelings about these disagreements her voice became more overtly angry. When I pointed this out, she denied that she was angry but admitted that she was "irritated" with her husband over a number of issues that she had been reluctant to raise previously. He was obsessed with his work. He didn't spend enough time with the family. He was too strict with Adam. He drank too much and he was attentive to her only when he wanted sex.

In the third session, John and Alice admitted that their marriage was tense and that they needed help with their relationship. Adam's behavior problems at home were the result of his distress over his parents' angry arguments and his splitting them to his own advantage by appealing to his mother when his father set limits he didn't want to follow. As John and Alice worked on their communications, grew to understand each other better, to be more responsive to each other's needs, and to agree on discipline for Adam, Adam settled down. Without my recognizing and helping to resolve the subtle anger of his parents, Adam's problem might not have been addressed properly.

I have been impressed by the number of creative euphemisms people use to express various degrees of their anger while simultaneously denying it. Alice wasn't angry with her husband, she was "irritated" with him. I have heard other people say, "I'm not angry, I'm just frustrated." "I'm not angry with my husband, I'm disappointed in him." Or, "I'm unhappy with him." I have compiled a partial list of synonyms people use for varying degrees of anger, from mild irritation to rage: frustrated, disappointed, unhappy, upset, dismayed, exasperated, bitter, discouraged, disillusioned, disgruntled, irritated, offended, annoyed, bothered, pissed off, ticked off, put off, turned off, displeased, disturbed, perturbed, provoked, rankled, incensed, resentful, indignant, irked, riled, ruffled, steamed, peeved, and piqued. The thesaurus gives the antonyms as: composed, calm, soothing, kind, reconciling, and loving.

If the anger is an evanescent spark without aggression or the intent to hurt, and it is over and forgotten quickly, it is harmless. Usually, when the anger persists, there are problems not being addressed, often because one or both people are afraid to address them. When it is hot and abusive or cold and chronic, anger can destroy personal friendships and marriages. In forty years of practicing psychotherapy, I have counseled many couples. In every case the marriage or relationship was threatened or destroyed by anger—either cold anger that smoldered in subtle resentment and emotional withdrawal or hot anger that burst into aggression and abuse.

The issues underlying the anger were less important than the anger itself. Couples may conflict over many sensitive issues—money, sex, time, children, in-laws, politics, religion, and so on. The critical factor for the survival of the relationship is the emotional tone of the interaction. I have known happily married people of different social class, religion, race, and political beliefs. Their marriage survived because they discussed and worked patiently on their conflicts with mutual respect. I have also known otherwise compatible couples whose marriage was destroyed by anger over apparently trivial issues, such as how to furnish a house. When anger is acted out aggressively in word and deed, egos are wounded and hurt. Bruised egos wall themselves up, become closed and cold, and retaliate defensively with equally hurtful resentment, anger, and aggression, thus perpetuating the cycle of mutual destruction.

We usually think of anger as manifesting as person against person conflicts. But groups can be angry at groups. Groups can be angry at individuals. And individuals can be angry at groups. Religious, ethnic, and other passionate wars are often ignited by anger and fueled with frustrated, chauvinistic pride—the desire of a group to survive, to prosper, and to dominate. Human groups, like human individuals, must construct and preserve their identities. Wars between states, ethnic groups, religious factions, even neighbors are, ultimately, motivated by the quest for a solid, secure identity. When I remind my patients that their conflicts resemble national struggles, they laugh—but they understand. It may seem odd to compare nations to people, but reading national conflicts through what we know about identity and subjectivity can be illuminating.

The Israelis and the Palestinians, for example, have long suffered from the bitter fruits of hatred, aggression, and violence. The Palestinians want land and a secure state of their own in order to establish and preserve their ethnic-religious identity. The Israelis also want a secure state which preserves Jewish identity. They fear being attacked and outnumbered by their adversaries, some of whom are violently anti-Israel. Many disputes must be resolved but—as in a marriage, a family, or a workplace—peace will come not when each side gets all of what it wants but when each side gives up some of what it wants.

The scapegoat is a sacrifice of another for the benefit of self. Anti-Semitism illustrates the classical meaning of the scapegoat. Many aboriginal peoples understood, in ways that we do not, that the universe feeds on itself, an idea which is represented in the icon of Uroboros, the snake who eats its own tail. Primitive ritual sacrifice was an offering to a bloodthirsty god or cosmos in the hope of a barter in which the blood of the group would be spared.

In modern times, hatred is most strongly felt by those who are confused, uncertain, or dissatisfied with their own social identity. The Holocaust was a sacrifice of the Jews in order to establish a "pure" Aryan identity. Similarly, discrimination against blacks is a form of scapegoating in the service of establishing a "pure" white identity. The key here is to understand the tenacity of the quest for identity and its relationship to anger, aggression, and violence. As we become aware of this interplay in history, we become more aware of it in our own private lives.

The dialectics of scapegoating are at one end of a continuum of discriminations between the me and the not-me which, at the other end, includes normal identity formation. The "me" can be me as opposed to my mother; my mother and me as opposed to my father; my family as opposed to my neighbor's family; my school versus another school; my state, my religion, my national identity against the Other. An old mid-Eastern proverb expresses the vicissitudes of identity: "I against my brother; I and my brother against my cousin; I and my cousin against the next village."

Aboriginal communities often divided themselves into "binary moieties" to establish distinct identities within a common culture. Similar binary moieties can be seen today in college and professional team sports. The Yankees and the Mets derive their identities as adversaries in the same game of organized baseball. The sense of self depends on a sense of Other and cannot be created or sustained except in relation to the Other. One can identify with the Other when there is harmony and a common purpose. The two become "a couple" and the group becomes a "we." When there is disharmony and a conflict of interest, the Other, on whom we depend for our identity, must be rejected, dominated, or conquered. As we have noted, the basic cause of human anger, aggression, and violence lies in the instinct for survival sublimated into the desire for a meaningful, enduring identity.

Christ, Galileo, and Martin Luther King were all individuals hated by groups. Christ was condemned because he threatened Jewish orthodoxy and Roman hegemony. Galileo was condemned by the Catholic Church for advocating a heliocentric (sun at the center) view of the universe, contrary to the Church's dogmatic geocentric (Earth at the center) view. By threatening traditional Catholic cosmology, Galileo was perceived as threatening the Church's credibility and authority. He was brought to trial and sentenced to silence under the threat of being burned at the stake as a heretic. Martin Luther King was hated and murdered by white supremacists and racists who perceived him as a threat to their dominance. The irony is that we cannot vanquish the Other because we *depend* on the Other for our sense of ourselves. Kill him and he will rise again, like Phoenix, and often with our own help, as we saw with the Marshall Plan after World War II and as we see in Iraq today. Self and other are bound together like in and out. To lose another is to lose part of one's self. They are a dialectical pair inseparably joined in an unstable marriage of minds.

In our own conflicts with others, the root of our anger can be difficult to pin down and thus, resolve. Different emotions are often packed into each other, with one emerging as dominant while others are hidden but potent. Anger can hide anxiety, depression, guilt, envy, and jealousy as well as being hidden by them.

Roberta consulted me because of acute anxiety. When we reviewed her life situation it was obvious that her greatest stress was her conflict with her boss. I detected anger in her voice when she spoke about him, and I asked if she was angry at him. She paused for a moment, as if surprised by her discovery. "I'm furious at him," she replied. "I hate how he treats me. But what can I do? I'm afraid that if I get angry with him, he'll fire me." She complained that her boss was rude, hypercritical, derisive, and disrespectful towards her but she was afraid to express it because she depended on him for her job, for her livelihood. The anxiety was the presenting complaint, but the underlying problem was anger.

Roberta was anxious because she was afraid of her own anger. From childhood she had been demanding, hot-tempered, and given to outbursts of anger. Her parents loved her and tolerated her anger. Her husband left her because of it. Now she was in a situation in which she felt she must either endure humiliation, the painful diminishment of her own sense of identity, or become angry and lose her job. As she explored her anger, she became more aware of the issues that troubled her. She did not gracefully endure the frustration of her will.

I suggested that there may be merit in her grievances but that her anger made it impossible to address them constructively. I quoted an old Tibetan proverb: "The wise person knows that you catch more flies with honey than with vinegar." I asked her to examine her assumption that her boss didn't like her, that his rudeness was a personal attack on her. After all, he had given her generous raises every year. He wrote glowing evaluation reports of her. True, he was rude and offensive in his manner. Perhaps her willfulness was sometimes inadvertently offensive to him. Could she see this as possibly his problem and not hers? I asked her if she would reconsider her belief that her boss thought she was a bad person and consider the possibility that he might be insensitive and unaware of his effect on others.

She reflected on this advice and began to examine and challenge her assumptions. After a while, noting her progress, I suggested that she might try to talk with her boss in a neutral, friendly setting and try to make him aware of how he upset her. We also considered the dangers of doing this. She might lose control of herself, become angry, and offend him. He might have a grievance against her that she didn't know about. Making such a choice, like many choices, could be productive or disastrous.

I worked with Roberta on ways and means to calm her body and mind from the agitating effects of anger and anxiety. After a long period of reflection and practice of the methods, Roberta decided to talk with her boss. She invited him to have a cup of coffee with her. Following my suggestion, rather than rebuking him, she asked for his sympathy and help. Her boss turned out to be a decent person. He was surprised and shocked. He hadn't realized that her feelings were hurt by his behavior. He offered what seemed to be a sincere apology and thanked her for confronting him so diplomatically. He told her that his wife also complained that he was sometimes too blunt and rude. He said that he didn't want to offend his employees, that he valued her contributions and wanted her to continue to work with him. Her relationship with her boss became more honest, cordial, and mutually respectful, which benefited them both.

Roberta's anxiety was fear of her own anger. She didn't conquer her willfulness or her anger in this course of therapy, but she was able to control herself well enough to relate to the situation constructively. Not every polite confrontation will end so happily. Some people are narcissistically insensitive to the feelings of others. Her boss could have become defensively aggressive towards her, perhaps provoking her anger, in which case the confrontation might have ended in disaster. Life is dangerous.

Anger often lies hidden beneath depression. I am convinced that anxiety, anger, and depression are closely related. They are all fueled by the energy of our desires and aversions. Anxiety and anger are fight-flight responses to the perception of danger—namely, the danger that one's desires will be frustrated and the unwanted will be imposed. Anxiety is the experience of mental flight without physical flight. Anger is the experience of mental fight without physical fight. Underlying both anxiety and anger is a feeling of helplessness. The main features of depression are feelings of helplessness and hopelessness. Depression is anger without hope and, therefore, without passion. When people feel helpless they are likely to experience anxiety and anger. When they also feel hopeless, they become depressed.

Emily consulted me for depression. As she related her history, she mentioned vaguely that there were problems in her marriage. In the second session, I asked her about her marriage. She complained that her husband, Jim, was dominating, demanding, occasionally verbally abusive, and useless around the house. On the other hand, they had three children and a nice home. He was a good provider and she loved him, his inconsiderate behavior notwithstanding. She didn't want to divorce him and break up her family, yet she was unhappy and felt hopeless that she would be any happier in the future. She began to cry spontaneously, to lose interest in her domestic life, and to lose her sexual desire. She developed insomnia and anorexia, classic symptoms of depression. When she came to see me, she had lost twenty pounds over six months. She believed she was suffering from a chemical imbalance and asked for Prozac.

I told her I needed to know more about her before I would prescribe an anti-depressant. I asked her if she was angry with her husband. She admitted that she was, in a soft, childish, helpless voice. But what could she do? She had vented her anger at her husband. She had complained to him about his behavior. She had asked him to change. Sometimes he would agree but he never followed up. At other times he angrily accused her of nagging him. I suggested that her depression might be the result of her feelings of helplessness and hopelessness about her marriage. If she could get in touch with her anger and the frustrations that generated it, perhaps she could confront her husband in a more consistent, persistent, and constructive manner and actually create change.

She brightened perceptibly at the hope for change. Her depression lifted when she got in touch with her anger and sublimated it into an energetic, hopeful determination to create a positive change in her life. She talked with her husband and explained to him that her depression was the result of her feeling hopeless that he would change and treat her with more respect. At first he was dismissive and defensive. He denied that he treated her badly and made excuses. I suggested that she ask him to join us for a therapy session. He agreed, and at that meeting he expressed concern about his wife's mental state. I explained to him that her depression was the result of her frustrations, her anger, and her feelings of helplessness and hopelessness. I asked if he would meet with me alone. He agreed. He loved his wife, he said, and would do anything for her.

I began the session with Jim gently in order to develop some trust and rapport. I didn't want him to feel blamed or pressured. We talked generally about problems that men and women have with each other. I casually mentioned that his wife felt ignored, disrespected and, sometimes, abused. At first he was defensive and complained about her. He worked hard to support her, he said, and she was sometimes demanding, argumentative, and neglectful. But he loved his wife and didn't want to lose her.

He called for another appointment and told me that he had been thinking about our last meeting. He wanted more clarity about what was going on between Emily and him. They had been tense with each other. They were not making love or having much fun together. As he examined his thoughts and behavior he began to see how he did expect her to take care of him and the house. He felt that since he brought home the money to pay the mortgage, she should serve him. Not an unconventional idea except that he was forgetting that they had three children and Emily was a full-time mother. She sometimes needed help and couldn't always be there for him when she had to care for the children.

To his credit, Jim began to reflect on his expectations and feelings. He could see that he was angry at Emily for not meeting his needs, and sometimes lost his temper and became abusive. I asked him if he had ever taken care of the children for a day. He had not. I suggested that he try it sometime. Maybe it would help him to understand his wife and show some compassion.

Emily thought it was a great idea! The next weekend, he tried it. Emily took a day off to visit with friends. Jim had the children for a day—an eight-year-old boy, a six-year-old boy, and a two-year-old girl. At the next session, he confessed to feeling humbled. He hadn't realized how difficult Emily's job was. The children consumed his full attention. He couldn't let them out of his sight for a minute. He could see how difficult Emily's life was and how he was being self-righteously demanding and childishly angry. He thought he had better make some changes.

With the help of our talks, Jim made a conscious, deliberate decision to be more attentive to Emily, to hear her out, to talk more gently, and to show respect. He followed through. He began to do some chores around the house, but he did them reluctantly and with some resentment. I asked him why he was resentful. Was he voluntarily choosing to do the chores or did he feel forced or intimidated? He didn't have to do them. But then he would have to deal with Emily's resentment. How long would their marriage last in an atmosphere of cool tension? It was his choice. I told him that if he was going to choose to do some chores, he should choose wholeheartedly and not hold back out of spiteful pride. As he consciously took responsibility for his choice, his resentment disappeared. As their relationship improved, Emily's depression began to lift, and she began to sleep better and gain weight. Their sex life revived and they began to take occasional weekend honeymoon vacations together.

When she came to therapy complaining of depression, Emily was unaware that her primary problem was anger at Jim. Jim's anger was often hidden by his coldness towards Emily and his unwillingness to help her. They were able to heal their anger because they took all Seven Steps without being aware that they had taken even one. They were willing to examine themselves, to become aware of their anger and its consequences, to see their relationship in a different light, to open to each other, and to take responsibility and make different choices.

5. Step Two: Taking Responsibility

As you develop awareness of your anger in its various manifestations and disguises, the next step is to take complete and total responsibility for it. This is the most difficult step and the most crucial. Without taking full responsibility for your anger, no healing is possible. This step is difficult because we think our anger is caused by an external situation or by a problem with our brain chemistry.

Our natural tendency is to justify our anger by blaming someone or something else. Someone betrayed us, obstructed our desires, interfered with our plans, dashed our hopes, or was insensitive. Or, the weather was bad, the stock market fell, or an accident made us late. Isn't our anger justified? Isn't it caused by an external event? If the event didn't happen we wouldn't have gotten angry. How can we take responsibility for it? What does that mean?

To think that an external event *causes* our anger is a mistake. It leaves something vital out of the equation. The external event is a *factor* in our anger, but not the cause. Our desires and aversions are directed outward. We want events to go our way. We want others to promote our interests and not interfere. But we have failed to consider that *the essence of our humanity is discriminating awareness and discriminating choice.* We have a choice in how we judge and how we respond to others and to external events. We have failed to consider *our* role–our minds, our attitudes, our desires and aversions, our judgments, our self-centeredness, and our ability and willingness to control ourselves. What is left out is *mind* as an intermediate agent between external events and the energy of anger. Depending on our state of mind, we may become angry at the most trivial inconvenience or rest in equanimity in the most horrible bad fortune.

To take full responsibility for our anger, two main obstacles must be overcome and two sacrifices made. The first obstacle is the temptation to blame other people or circumstances. We all want to feel right about ourselves and justified in our actions. Placing the blame outside of ourselves helps us feel justified. The blame both expresses our anger and justifies it. "She did it to me! Look what he did! See what happened? How can you blame me for being angry?" We have a bounty of things to blame: other people (and plenty of them provoke us, including our family, friends, and lovers); social conditions or institutions (e.g. poverty, injustice, prejudice, intrusive government, corrupt corporations, etc.); and a widely used causal scapegoat, mental illness. As previously discussed, many experts now blame past emotional traumas, genetic defects, or neurochemical imbalances for outbursts of anger, aggression, and violence. Blaming our anger on one of these factors, however, will serve only to justify and perpetuate it.

No matter what social or biological factors are involved, ultimately we must take responsibility for our anger, aggression, and violence. So the first sacrifice is to renounce blaming as a way of soothing our egos. This emphatically does not mean that others haven't acted wrongly or haven't done us harm, or that outer events are not unfortunate or tragic. *It means that our intention is to work on our anger no matter what the provocation.* Blaming others may *seem* justified when the offense is outrageous. Even then, to the degree that we blame others and fail to take responsibility for our anger, we cripple our ability to heal it. This is a very difficult obstacle to overcome. The tendency to blame is almost instinctive. The key is to keep working at it.

The second obstacle is our unwillingness to examine ourselves. Our natural tendency is to exaggerate our virtues and minimize our faults and flaws because we want to feel good about ourselves.

How can we feel good about ourselves if *we* are the cause of our anger rather than external events? Doesn't this mean that we are to blame? If we get angry at someone who interferes with us, who does us harm, who steals from us, lies to us, or betrays us, does taking responsibility for our anger mean blaming ourselves rather than the thief, the liar, or the traitor? We think that if others are not to blame for our anger then we must be. This is the logic of blame. We are still playing the blame game. Self-blame is, ironically, motivated by the desire to feel good about ourselves. Self-condemnation is a display of conscience. By confessing our guilt we are showing that we know right from wrong and admitting that we have done wrong. At the same time, we are excusing others, perhaps hoping that they will forgive us. In Anglo-American law a confession of guilt usually leads to a degree of mercy, a lighter sentence, and, sometimes, praise.

The second sacrifice is to give up blaming yourself. Taking responsibility does not mean blaming yourself. On the contrary, it means not blaming yourself *or* anyone else. This can be tricky. It does *not* mean *not* looking at your part in generating anger. It means looking at yourself without quickly judging or defending yourself. Instead, just look at your thoughts, feelings, and actions and their consequences dispassionately, including being aware of what you want or don't want to happen. This does not mean that we abandon the capacity to make moral distinctions. On the contrary, it may help us to understand them more deeply and to see our own desires and fears more clearly. This lesson often has to be learned over and over again before it can be deeply understood and integrated. We all have the capacity to be aware of ourselves, to acknowledge our desires and aversions without blaming ourselves, and to know whether what we do is harmful to ourselves or others.

The word "responsibility" can be very confusing because it is used in many contradictory ways. Often, people use it to mean blameworthy, as when an accused is found responsible for a crime and thus guilty, accountable, and justly punishable. "You are responsible" can be interpreted to mean: "It's your fault, you are to blame, and you deserve to be punished." In this case, the jury blames the responsible person and, except for certain excusing conditions, rejects the idea that other people or external events are the cause of his actions. The function of this sense of "responsibility" is to provide a rationale for judgment and punishment.

Another popular meaning of responsibility is "obligation." "You are responsible for doing your chores." "The class will be responsible for turning their papers in on time." "You are responsible for driving carefully." Freedom is tolerable only when there is a common restraint on it. This restraint is called "responsibility" and is defined as a virtue. "Responsibility," in this sense, is a restriction on the satisfaction of certain desires and requirement to face certain aversions, like taxes, for example. "With freedom comes responsibility, and the responsibility of the citizen is to obey the law." The function of this sense of the word is to persuade, to obligate, and to coerce. Neither of these two meanings of the word will be used here.

In the sense in which it is used here, the word "responsibility" means "response-ability," that is, the ability to respond with a variety of constructive choices rather than merely to react out of impulse or conditioning. Responsibility is an acquired skill, like learning chess, except here it refers to learning to live intelligently and skillfully. Anger usually erupts as an immediate, unplanned, unintended, automatic reaction to a person or a situation to which we are averse. It is fueled by insistent desires, implacable fears, or inflexible aversions which may or may not be conditioned by past experiences. Taking responsibility means refusing the tyranny of automatic or habitual reactions and, instead, cultivating a willingness to accept some degree of frustration, anxiety, and helplessness. It means learning to tolerate unpleasant or painful experiences without impulsively acting to reduce them in a manner which may be negative or harmful to yourself or others. It means reflecting on the situation and responding to it with positive, constructive action or with inaction. The wise Buddhist nun, Pema Chodron, advises her students:

> Right at the point you are about to blow your top, remember this: You are a disciple being taught how to sit still with the edginess and discomfort of the energy. You are a disciple being challenged to hold your seat and open to the situation with as much courage and kindness as you possibly can.

Taking responsibility means accepting authorship and ownership of your thoughts, feelings, and actions, and their consequences. This may seem like a radical proposal. It seems to be asking too much, but we have the capacity to accept responsibility for our *behavior.* Social etiquette, rules, and laws stipulate that we do so. We could not live together if we did not. *But our thoughts and feelings, too?* We often regard them as beyond our conscious control. Our thoughts and feelings seem to come upon us unbidden. We think that they *seize* us. How can we be responsible for thoughts which pop into our minds and feelings which arise without our willing them?

We have all been through mind training in school. Mathematics is mind training. In math we learn to control our thinking and follow very precise procedures. In school we learn to control our bodies in sport. We learn to read and write and, therefore, to think. Learning grammar is mind training. At home, we can allow our emotions to flow more freely and sometimes, to rage. But at school or at work we must control ourselves. If we have the ability to be responsible for our thoughts and feelings some of the time, don't we have that potential more of the time?

Accepting ownership means acknowledging that the causes and, thus, the power to control our thoughts, feelings, and actions, including anger and aggression, lie within us rather than in other people or outer situations. "Within us" means within our own minds. Taking responsibility for our anger means realizing that anger is a function of mind. It means looking into it, seeing for ourselves, and knowing through our own experience that other people and outer circumstances cannot control our mind unless we allow them to. With awareness, we can see for ourselves that external events will provoke us only to the degree that we allow ourselves to be provoked. Anger can only be healed through transforming the mind's response.

Ellen was a twenty-one-year-old college student who came to therapy for depression which prevented her from concentrating on her schoolwork. Her grades were falling and she was faced with the possibility of having to drop out of school. She gave a history of having been sexually abused by her father from the time she was eight years old until she was thirteen, when she resisted her father's assaults and he withdrew from her. The abuse consisted of her father fondling her genitals and forcing her to touch his penis. He threatened to accuse her of lying if she revealed the abuse to her mother. Her sister, two years older, recently told her that she had also been sexually abused by her father.

Ellen was extremely angry with her father but had always been afraid to confront him. She complained about it to her mother after the abuse had stopped, but her mother denied that her husband could have committed such a horrible act and refused to confront him for fear that it would destroy their marriage and break up the family. From the time she left home for college, Ellen avoided going home for holidays and vacations because of her unresolved anger towards her father. As a result, she became isolated from her mother, sister, and brother, whom she loved and missed very much. Her depression was the result of her suppressed, futile anger towards her father and her grieving for her lost family.

As Ellen got in touch with her anger and was able to express it, her depression began to lift. Motivated by her outrage, she became preoccupied with the idea of going home for the Christmas holidays for the first time in three years and confronting her father. As she rehearsed the confrontation in her mind, she began to hesitate out of fear of hurting her mother and breaking up her family. As she struggled with the conflict, she asked me for advice on whether to confront her father or not. I advised her that the choice was hers and that she should consider her feelings and the possible consequences of each course of action. But whether she chose to confront her father or not, she should first look at her anger and try to heal it.

The idea that healing her anger was important *for her* was extremely difficult for her to accept, understandably, because she felt that her father had committed an unforgivable act and that her anger was justified. How could she forgive him? I agreed that her father's actions were inexcusable and that her anger was understandable. Nevertheless, she was suffering from her unresolved anger and she might better be able to make a decision if she examined her anger more closely and took responsibility for it. To forgive her father is not to excuse him. *Forgiveness is for the forgiver.* It is an acceptance of things as they were and are. Ellen experienced a small epiphany when she began to reflect on my suggestion that there was a difference between taking responsibility for her anger and excusing her father for his actions. Her father's actions were abominable. Nevertheless, her anger was hers.

As she examined her anger she realized that she harbored the hidden wish that the abuse had not happened. It was as if her anger enabled her to hold on to the hope that it would all go away. When she was depressed, she had given up hope it would go away because the trauma was continually present in her yearning for the family she was avoiding. As she got angrier, hope returned, but it was a hopeless hope. To heal her anger, Ellen had to face the facts. She, like all of us, had to accept the irreversibility of the past. The facts of the abuse and her emotional response to the abuse could not be denied or reversed. They were unchangeable historical facts. She, like all of us, had the choice of accepting the past, accepting that the abuse had happened, or being continuously caught up, motivated by, and projecting into her life all the tangled emotions connected to the impossible wish that it hadn't happened.

Ellen also realized that she was angry because she was afraid of her father and her fear made her feel helpless to confront him, and ashamed. Gradually, she began to understand the difference between excusing her father for his actions and accepting that they had occurred. She realized that she had harbored the fantasy that by confronting her father, the fact of the abuse would be undone. As she accepted the *fact* that he had abused her, she began to relax and release her anger while still maintaining her view that her father was guilty of an inexcusable act. As she came in touch with her fear of her father she realized it would take courage to confront him. And as she mustered the courage, her self-esteem improved.

As she took responsibility for her anger it began to subside. I have seen this remarkable change often when people take responsibility for their anger. They begin to soften and relax into their pain. If the danger is within ourselves, it is not as threatening as if it comes from outside. As we take responsibility for our anger we are confronted with choices. As Ellen struggled with the choice of whether or not to confront her father, she felt the pain of both decisions. If she confronted him, she would feel guilty for hurting and, possibly, fracturing her family. If she did not, she would feel ashamed of her cowardice all of her life.

I advised her to consider the difference between what Buddhists call "true and false guilt." True guilt is a feeling of remorse for having intentionally hurt someone else or having broken a law. False guilt is the fear that someone will feel hurt by something you say or authentically do with no desire to harm them. False guilt makes us inauthentic. It motivates us to act in such a way that we think people will like us or, at least, not reject us. Confronting her father would be an authentic act because the intent is not to harm but to expose a dark secret, to acknowledge an injustice, to open an opportunity for confession and, perhaps, even forgiveness. As she reflected on the difference between hurting her family and their being hurt by the revelation of her past, she felt empowered.

As therapy progressed, Ellen began to realize that she could choose to accept the fact that she was abused by her father without excusing him for his actions. She could see the value of confronting him without anger, in that it would present him with the opportunity to confess and ask forgiveness or deny everything and live a lie. This also gave her a feeling of empowerment. While she was angry she was afraid to confront him, afraid her anger would become the issue rather than the abuse. If she was not angry her father would be on the spot, not her. She also got in touch with her desires to be close to the rest of her family whom she missed terribly.

As she realized it was her decision and that she could choose to confront her father or not, her anger subsided and her depression lifted. As she thought about it, she wavered from one choice to the other, reflecting on the possible consequences of each. Finally, she decided that she was strong enough to choose to accept the past without anger. She felt able to confront her father but chose to spare her family the pain. She decided to visit her family and enjoy them and to remain cordial but emotionally distant from her father.

The next week, she reported that the visit went well. She was very happy to reconnect with her mother and siblings and she discovered that she could see her father in a new way, not angrily, as a demon, but compassionately as a deeply flawed, sad, emotionally closed man with whom she couldn't and didn't want to feel close, but was no longer angry at. By taking responsibility for her anger and for her decision to accept the past without excusing or confronting her father, she felt a new sense of self-esteem and mastery. She was soon able to refocus on her schoolwork and she graduated with honors.

The crucial step for Ellen's healing was not that she decided not to confront her father. Other victims of abuse might choose confrontation and feel just as good about it. The choice is up to the individual. No expert can take that "responsibility." The important point is that whichever choice the victim of abuse makes, the path of healing lies in taking responsibility for the anger—that is, acknowledging and utilizing the capacity to choose the response. Deciding not to confront her father while remaining angry at him would not have healed Ellen's depression and pain. Choosing to confront him out of anger would more likely lead to an unhappy cycle of hurt, cold defensiveness, hurtful offensiveness, continuing anger, and depression. The path of healing anger begins with taking responsibility for it.

Sometimes people don't take responsibility for their anger and they continue to live in pain. Fred consulted me under duress. He was a thirty-seven-year-old successful carpenter and house builder, a Vietnam veteran who saw bloody action. He was a "macho" man, big and muscular, rode motorcycles and liked to drink beer and go hunting and fishing with his male friends. He didn't really want to see a therapist, but his wife insisted. In fact, she threatened to leave him if he didn't see a therapist about his anger. The week before he came to see me he had lost his temper and slapped her across the face. He was sorry he had done it. He admitted it was wrong. "But she provoked me, doc. I mean, I'm sorry I did it. I don't want to hurt her. I love her. She's a good wife and mother to my kids. But she provokes me. She gets in my face."

I asked him if he got angry with his wife often and what he got angry about. He told me that it started out as a little thing, but then grew until they were having hot arguments once or twice a week or more, usually, he said with self-satisfied cynicism, "over me seeing my friends. I told her from the beginning–my friends are important to me. I like to spend time with them. She gets jealous. She doesn't want me to. She wants me home with her and the kids every night. I have a right to see my friends, don't I doc?"

I sensed that he was asking me to authorize his anger by confirming that it was justified. If I agreed with him, then he could go home and tell his wife that his anger was her fault. And if I disagreed with him he would have sized me up as siding with his wife. I avoided this trap by telling him that I would like to discuss that with him but that I felt there was a prior problem, namely his anger and abuse of his wife. I asked him, "Do you want to continue to be angry with your wife and create a crisis in your marriage? Or do you want to learn to manage your anger more effectively, no matter whether I agree with you or not about your conflict with your wife? Whether you have the right to see your friends or not is, ultimately, for you to decide. You have to consider the consequences of whatever choice you make. But you have no right to hit your wife. And your anger at her is eroding your relationship with her, which you say is important to you. Do you want to work on your anger?"

He was caught between his love of his wife and his attachment to his friends. He didn't want to give up either. He agreed to work on his anger, but insincerely and with hesitation. He agreed for the self-serving reasons that it would satisfy his wife's demand that he see a therapist and it would buy time to see whether he could get out of this without having to go through changes. Nevertheless, he had not shut the door tightly on working on his anger and agreed to continue to talk with me for a while, "if it'll help," he added, reminding me of his option to quit whenever he wanted to. "Whether it helps or not is up to you," I replied. He made another appointment.

At the second session, I asked him to tell me about his anger—its history from as far back as he can remember, any patterns he could see, the worst instances of it, how he felt about it. As he talked he became aware of the crucial role of anger in his life. Hearing himself tell his own story, he realized that there was a trail of anger and aggression leading back to his father's anger and aggression towards his mother and himself. He could see his father in himself. And he could see the problems anger had created in his life–with his parents, in school where he got into a few fights, with friends with whom he had conflicts, with his superiors in the military and other authority figures, and now with his wife.

I asked him if he wanted to continue to manifest his anger, considering that it may cost him his marriage, or did he want to deal with it? Was he willing to commit himself to mastering it? "How do I do that?" he asked skeptically. "I'll show you," I replied. "But first you must take responsibility for your anger and look at it. If you do that, you can learn to manage it. If you don't do that, if you won't accept that challenge, then the course of your life may be shaped by your anger and you may suffer greatly from it." He muttered skeptically and finally said, "I love my wife, doc. I don't want to lose her. She's the best thing that has ever happened to me. I'll do whatever it takes."

With Fred's permission, I interviewed his wife, Karen. She began by recounting to me in an angry voice the incident in which Fred slapped her. "I'm not going to stand for being physically abused," she declared. "Once more and he's outta there. Also, I'm tired of his not being home. I don't like it that he spends so much time with his friends. I'm jealous, I admit it. But I want a home life, a husband who wants to be with his family. Not an adolescent who wants to jock around with his male friends and do whatever he wants. If he doesn't change, I don't know how long our marriage will last." Her anger softened into sadness and she began to cry. "But I love him. He's a good man. He means well. I know he loves me. He loves his kids. He's a good provider. When he's home, we all have a good time together. It's a good life with him some of the time. I don't want to lose him. But I won't stand for being beaten, abused, or disrespected."

At the next session with Fred, I asked him his side of the story. Why did he hit his wife? "I'm sorry I did that, doc. I told you that. But she gets in my face. She tries to control me. I guess I reached my limit and exploded at her. I don't want to be controlled. I hate it when people tell me what to do. She wants me to live my life her way. I'm not going to give up my buddies. They're my buddies."

"It sounds to me like you're blaming your anger on your wife," I replied. He stumbled for words. "Yeah! She shouldn't get in my face and she shouldn't try to control me. She pisses me off when she won't make love unless I do what she wants." I was quick to answer. "Now is the time to honor your commitment to take responsibility for your anger. How are *you* causing your anger?" "Me? How am I? What do you mean?" "Well," I replied, "we get angry when we're not getting what we want or we're getting what we don't want." "Right!" he shouted. "I want to hang out with my friends without Karen getting angry with me."

"Maybe you can't have both," I replied. "You can't control Karen. She may decide that she would rather be single than live with an absentee, abusive husband. And she can't control you. You can continue to see your friends whenever you want, or you can honor Karen's desire for you to be home more. It's your choice. You are responsible for making that choice. To get angry with your wife because you don't want to be faced with the choice, and to try to bully her into seeing things your way, is not taking responsibility for your anger or yourself."

He suddenly sobered. In a flash he saw that he was trying to control Karen with has anger into letting him do whatever he wanted, but driving her away in the process. Over several sessions it became clear to him that taking responsibility for his anger meant that he had to make a choice. He had to respect Karen's feelings and not try to change them by intimidation and force. That meant that he had to choose between his wife and family and his friends. His friends were mostly single, or divorcing, or also in troubled relationships. The guys with good marriages came around less often and spent more time with their families.

We spent several sessions discussing his relationship and relationships in general. We discussed how marriage is a merger of two people in which, if it is to last, each must surrender a degree of individuality for the sake of creating a common ground. Surrender means the surrender of normal, neurotic mind fiercely defending its own territory, its own likes, dislikes, and sense of self. A loving relationship requires a softening and an opening of heart to heart. It is a dance of giving and receiving.

It is a delicate dance. One cannot give up everything and become stuck to the other like glue lest one lose one's self and the respect of the other, too. Relationships can feel suffocating if they are not spacious. Yet, as each attempts to find a sense of individuality, conflicts may arise which erupt into anger, aggression, or violence. In every relationship, people have the contradictory desires to merge with the other and to be separate from the other. People go to extremes, from radical individuality with little willingness to surrender, to the other extreme of addiction to the other—a slave of pleasure, obligation, and guilt. In a good relationship, these polarities are in balance. "You have to work this out with Karen," I advised him, "in a way that each of you can live with, or you may not be able to live together."

Fred agreed to spend more time with his family, much to Karen's joy. But he did so in small steps, hesitantly, and with poorly hidden resentment. We examined how he was giving as little as possible, hoping to still have it his way, and reacting to his frustrations with variations of anger—reluctant cooperation, passive aggression, stinginess, a sharp tone of voice, and so on. After a few sessions, he saw how he was giving in gradually but grudgingly rather than openly and without resentment. He had not really committed himself to balancing his desires for time with his friends with his desire to honor Karen's wish that he be a full-time husband and father. As long as he was angry about the changes he was making, no matter how subtle, he was not taking responsibility for making a whole-hearted choice, without lingering resentment. Fred was not willing to take full responsibility for his anger. He cancelled appointments, drifted away, and eventually quit. I later learned that he and Karen continued to fight, grew apart, and eventually divorced.

The energy of anger cannot be tamed and transformed without taking responsibility for it. It would be like trying to ride a horse without mounting it. We must be careful, however, not to try to take responsibility as an obligation. It cannot be rigidly fixed as a set of rules, prescriptions, and prohibitions. Taking responsibility is a softening and an opening which permits flexible, creative choice. From the point of view of evolutionary biology, response-ability is an instrument of survival. I have always been amused by the term "natural selection" because it implies that nature chooses. And it does. It selects for survival those beings who are not stuck in one mode of reactivity. Responsibility is flexible, intelligent adaptation to a life situation. It can be a matter of survival for the individual as well as for the species.

6. Step Three: Understanding Anger, Aggression, and Violence

As you become more aware of your anger and take more responsibility for it, you will be able to see it more clearly and become familiar with features and dynamics of it that you had not seen before. The best way to become familiar with the energy of anger is to see for yourself. In fact, there is no other way. You can only ride the energy skillfully if you are intimate with it from your own experience.

In Chapter Three the practice of meditation was introduced as a means for recognizing and calming hypermentation. Once that calmer mind is established, you can begin to turn your attention to the actual content of thoughts and feelings. Once we have the reins in our hands, we can start to develop a working relationship with our untamed mind.

Allow yourself to settle down, using the techniques described in Chapter Three. When thoughts and feelings are arising more clearly and less frequently, and you are relaxed enough to observe them without becoming distracted or involved, then you are ready to turn your full attention to seeing how the energy of anger arises and unfolds.

You can perform this thought experiment in the comfort of your own home. When you are relaxed, recall the last time you became angry, or a vivid memory of having been angry in the past. Visualize the setting, the circumstances, and the people around you. Try to remember the situation just as a series of events, without allowing it to become a self-justifying or self-blaming story. If you feel your emotions rising as you remember, stop the experiment until they have cooled. It is very difficult to remember painful conflicts accurately. We all want to be able to respect and approve of ourselves. Remember, this work is not for the fainthearted.

Try to feel your way back into the situation. What happened? What did you feel? How did you react? What did you do and say? How did it work out? Why were you angry? Ponder these three critical questions: "What did I want that I didn't get?" "What was I getting that I didn't want?" "How did I feel about myself?" Remember these questions. Reflect on them. It takes a while to see more deeply into them. They are the key to understanding your anger. Pause here and reflect.

Everything that has been discussed so far can be summed up in this axiom: *The energy of anger is fueled by our desires, our aversions, and our self-interest.* (Refer to figure 1.) The more self-righteous and insistent are our desires and aversions, and the more vigorously we defend ourselves, the hotter the flames of anger will be. The more flexible we are, the more gracefully willing we are to give up what we want but cannot have and to open to what we don't want but cannot avoid, the more humble we are, the less likely we are to become angry, aggressive, or violent. This is the formula for turning the vinegar of anger into the honey of clarity and peace of mind.

In this exercise, try to clearly recall and identify the feelings that arose when you became angry. Again, don't judge, blame, or justify; simply acknowledge them. This is an important step. The more clearly we are aware of our feelings, the more skillfully we can work with them. The problem is that our desires and aversions are sometimes obvious and sometimes subtle and puzzling. Our physical desires are easy to recognize when they are frustrated. When we are hungry and become angry because the restaurant service is slow, it's not hard to figure out that our desire for food is being frustrated. When we are in a hurry and the traffic is slow, a little introspection will reveal that our desire is to drive faster and get to our destination more quickly. Physical desires are the easiest to identify, but they are the less frequent and more benign causes of anger. Our ego desires are trickier.

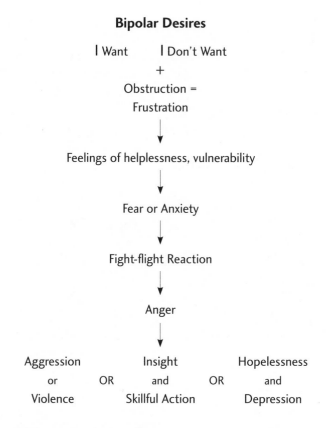

Bipolar Desires

I Want   I Don't Want
+
Obstruction =
Frustration

↓

Feelings of helplessness, vulnerability

↓

Fear or Anxiety

↓

Fight-flight Reaction

↓

Anger

↓

Aggression   Insight   Hopelessness
or   OR   and   OR   and
Violence   Skillful Action   Depression

FIGURE 1. THE DYNAMICS OF ANGER AND AGGRESSION

Ego desires are more abstract than physical desires. They are more sublime, more slippery and difficult to identify. We usually don't feel guilty about being hungry or sleepy, but we might be reluctant to admit that we love being admired, being cared for, and having our way. Admitting that these desires may be the motivations for our anger makes us uncomfortable. If you find yourself cringing a little as you become aware of these un-saintly desires and aversions, try to relax into the watcher's equanimity. You are a witness to human nature.

————————

Three ego desires require special attention and reflection. First, our expectations, our wishful ideas of how people and life should be, are a volatile ingredient in our mental and emotional life. We project our happiness projects into the future as ideal images that we count on. Inevitably, they will be tested by reality. Sometimes they will come true and sometimes they won't. Sometimes, our expectations are hidden by the language we use. Consider, for example, the concept of trust.

We want to trust the people in our lives. What does this mean? We think of trustworthiness as a quality of others. Some people can be trusted, others cannot. If we think about trust as a quality of our own, then it has a different twist. Trust is something we grant to others—depending on our confidence that we can predict how they behave. How can we trust an unpredictable person? He or she might do anything. A wife trusts that a husband will not be sexually unfaithful. If he is, her trust is broken. She becomes insecure. How can she be sure he won't betray her again? How can she rest in the expectation that he will be faithful in the future and not abandon her? This kind of trust is based on an illusion that breeds mistrust.

Some of our expectations are guaranteed by law. We expect that people won't steal, hurt, cheat, or kill us. If they do, the legal system will redress our grievance and impose a just penalty, which will discourage others from violating these expectations. But most of our expectations are informal, made up, a story we tell ourselves about how things should be, how we wish they would be, how they must be if we are to have the happy life we want and avoid trouble and pain.

We are bound to be angry when trust is broken. It threatens our happiness and makes us insecure and anxious. A wife will withdraw from a cheating husband. A boss will fire an employee who embezzles. Who will befriend the man who regularly breaks promises? From the point of view of our responsibility for our anger, however, the real problem is not in the person who violates our trust; the problem is in this kind of trusting, which is a disguised expectation.

This is not to say that the betrayed wife should not withdraw from the unfaithful husband if she chooses, or that we should befriend the promise-breaker or employ the embezzler. It is not to say that when our misplaced trust in others is violated we should blame our expectations and allow ourselves to be misused. Rather, it means that we must be willing to adjust our views to be congruent with reality and choose our responses with awareness and mature intelligence. It is difficult to be aware and intelligent if, to our disappointment, we add the misguided conviction that disappointment is an outrageous violation of the natural order of things. It is not.

A more reliable type of trust is trust in ourselves. This kind of trust is confidence (i.e., with faith) that we can relate responsibly to people and to the challenges of life *as they are*. The Tibetan word which is often translated as "neurosis" literally means "the failure to accept things as they are." The failure to accept people and life as they are is a powerful source of personal suffering. This does not mean that we should not pursue happiness and work for change for the better where possible. It means that there are aspects of life over which we have no control, and the greater wisdom is to accept the fact calmly. We must accept that we cannot control others, except as they voluntarily submit (and we will pay a price for their submission). We cannot entirely control the course of our lives. We may make choices, but their outcomes depend upon many outer factors. We may have total control over our input into life, but we have much less control than we wish over its outcome. Trust in ourselves is the confidence that we can deal with it.

We often become angry (or depressed) when life does not live up to our expectations. Our expectations function like unexamined, often unconscious, basic assumptions. We make all kinds of assumptions of how we should be, how others should be, and how life should be. One of the most prevalent, frequently unexamined assumptions in contemporary culture is the idea of progress, the idea that conditions will continuously improve. People take this idea personally. They expect more. They expect they will be able to move from a hut, to a shack, to an apartment, to a house, to a mansion. They want to move up from a Chevrolet to a Buick to a BMW, and retire at sixty-five. A professor friend of mine at Cornell University told me, with some dramatic hyperbole, that all his colleagues were depressed. I asked him why he thought they were depressed. He reflected for a moment and answered with a soft, knowing smile: "Because life hasn't turned out the way they thought it would."

We harbor expectations the way a path can harbor land mines. When life contradicts our idea of how things should be we often automatically respond with disappointment, anger, or depression. Disappointment is dashed expectation. It can disguise itself in many ways, especially as righteous indignation. If a man who gets angry at a slow waiter is not really hungry, then his anger wasn't fueled by the desire for food but by his desire to feel important and the expectation that he would be served promptly in accord with his high sense of himself. "I am a good person. I try to help others. I expect the courtesy of being served by others promptly and competently." He might even hide his ego desire, of which he may be somewhat ashamed, by claiming he is hungry even if he is not. This justifying subterfuge hides another, conflicting ego expectation: "I want to be viewed as a nice, good, unselfish, righteous person while I secretly pursue my desires, avoid the unwanted, and secure my sense of self." The ego is a trickster.

John, a thirty-three-year-old car salesman, consulted me because he was advised to seek psychiatric treatment for his mental illness. In the first session, he told me he had been diagnosed both as bipolar and as borderline and was heavily medicated. He adamantly insisted that he was not borderline. He felt misunderstood by previous psychiatrists. He had good reasons for his behavior, he said, which others did not understand. He also told me that he was angry with his father and that his life was a mess. As he revealed himself to me, I gradually reduced his medications until his mind was free of them.

After a few sessions, he told me he was able to think more clearly without the medication. As he talked about his life, it became apparent that he was in deep conflict with his father. His father called me and, with John's permission, I talked with him. His father told me about his own tumultuous life, including several marital disasters and a series of disruptive career successes and failures. A dynamic, intelligent, and now successful man, he could regret but not undo the fact that his own stormy life had affected his son. There had been setbacks, hard times, and mistakes. John had had to endure some disappointments.

John was a very forceful personality, to say the least. He was clever enough to defensively rationalize all of his unmet desires and expectations without being open to another point of view. He was convinced that his own suffering was caused by his father's failure to give him what he felt he was entitled to. He blamed his father for his troubles rather than taking responsibility for his life. In his youth he and his father had been in continuous conflict. When John was in his junior year of college, his father's business failed, he couldn't pay his son's tuition, and John dropped out of school. He entered and dropped out of a series of less prestigious colleges and never graduated. He always had a perfectly good excuse for his failures. His father didn't pay the tuition on time, the courses were not right for him, his social life was unsatisfactory, and so on. He had several "mental breakdowns" for which psychiatrists had prescribed medication which he blamed for his inability to function in school.

John came to see me after a particularly bad summer in which he continually fought with his father, threatened to kill him, and assaulted him physically. He tried to justify his anger by continually focusing on his father's flaws and failures. He complained that his father didn't understand him.

He was angry because he was not where he had expected to be in life. He was thirty-three years old and selling cars. He felt he was too old for the single women available to him in this college town. He couldn't find a girlfriend. He felt like a social outcast working for a peon's wage. Meanwhile, friends from college were doctors, lawyers, and businessmen making six-figure salaries, living in luxury apartments, and driving expensive cars. Out of jealousy and greed, he repeatedly bought luxurious items for himself and charged them to his father. He wanted the life his friends had. He expected to have it. He blamed his father for his disappointment. If it wasn't for his father he would be where he wanted to be in life, so he felt it was justifiable revenge to live as he "should" on his father's credit cards.

His father indulged him because he felt guilty about his life failures, especially his inability to pay his son's tuition. When John started therapy, he was unaware that his anger at his father was fueled and sustained by his intensely held expectations of what his life should be. He had been told he had some "illness," a mood disorder or a personality disorder which further reinforced his conviction that his anger and suffering were caused by afflictions unfairly visited upon him and beyond his control.

The root of his anger, however, was his unrealistic expectation that life would give him what he wanted. He spent more energy venting his anger at his father than he did solving life's problems as they arose. He might have pursued his dreams without his father's help, as many do. He could have taken a loan, finished college on his own, and gone on to graduate school or into the business world, as he wanted. He could have taken the real limitations inherent in his life situation into account and gracefully modified his expectations and demands. Had he taken responsibility for his anger, he may have been able to grasp the wisdom that no one's life turns out as they wish. Given that awareness, he might have discovered the bittersweet pleasure that comes with acceptance and adaptability, instead of wasting his life in frustration, rage, and self-defeating blame. The fault does not lie in life. It lies in the wish.

A wish is a desire with an ideational representation of its fulfill-ment. The wish to be rich is the desire for money and the desired things that money can buy. Expectations are wishes that we mis-takenly believe *should* and *must* be granted in the course of life. Unmasked, expectations are ideas about how people *should* act and how things *should* be. One can expose the idea, doubt the idea, and let go of it without completely letting go of the expectation. It remains as a wish, a desire for a state which has been rendered inchoate by the rejection of the idea, but which is, nevertheless, devoutly cherished. John came to see how his anger at his father was fueled by his expectation that he would be successful in life. He could admit it. He could explain his thoughts, feelings, and actions *ex post facto* as a manifestation of his expectations. He could even reconcile with his father. But he remained angry, not at his father, but at life itself because it had not granted his wishes and given him what he wanted.

———

The first ego desire fuels anger by responding to events through the filter of rigid expectations. The second ego desire, related to the first, is the wish for happiness. The difference between the two is that our expectations lie beneath the surface, awaiting the call to defend and justify the anger that follows inevitable disappoint-ment. Expectations require no effort. Pursuing happiness, on the other hand, requires effort, patience, and perseverance. The idea that our desire for happiness could be the cause of our anger seems to be an ego-twisting paradox. What's wrong with wanting to be happy? Everyone wants to be happy. It is the universal wish of humankind.

The problem is that we place conditions on our happiness. We will be happy "if...." We have ideas about what will make us happy and we have elaborate hopes and plans to achieve our dreams—our happiness projects. We want to end up in some kind of earthly or heavenly paradise where life is easy and pleasant. The mind is dialectical, however. It works through contrast, comparison, contradictions, paradoxes, and polarities. Up and down go together, as do right and left, self and other, and happiness and unhappiness. Understanding this polarity is a key to understanding the dynamics of the energy of anger.

If we think that money will make us happy, our most painful problems will be money problems. Every gain lifts our spirits, but every loss sinks them. Perhaps we believe that family life is the source of happiness. Surely, it can be the source of great happiness. But if a wonderful, smooth family life where everyone is happy with everyone all the time is our primary happiness project then our family problems will be the source of our worst pain.

Nowadays, we often refer to attachment as "addiction." Although that term originally referred to physical addiction, especially to drugs, its usage has become increasingly promiscuous. Now, it is said, we can become addicted to sex, to food, to gambling, to money, to TV, or even to people. These pleasures are called addictions because people suffer if the desire for them is unmet. In these terms, we can also become "addicted" to any of our happiness projects.

Osho tells the story of an old man who was the most unhappy man you could ever meet. He was so unhappy that people avoided him. They felt it would be impolite to be happy in his presence and did not want to feign unhappiness to be with him. One day, on his eightieth birthday, he woke up radiantly happy. His neighbors were surprised and puzzled. They gathered around him and said: "All your life you have been unhappy. You have been so unhappy we have avoided you just not to be infected with your sadness. Suddenly, you are radiant. What has happened?" The old man answered: "All my life I have been searching for happiness. Now that I am eighty years old, I realize my search has been futile. So I have given up."

The point of this story is not that we should give up our happiness projects in order to avoid unhappiness. It may be saintly, but it's not for us ordinary humans. Giving up a happiness project is itself a happiness project motivated by the desire to avoid pain. Yet pain cannot be avoided. Letting go is the better approach. The point of the story is to understand deeply that our cherished happiness projects may be frustrated and fail. We must learn to hold them, but loosely and lightly. We must be prepared to let go when we must, and to be more nimble and flexible in our approach to life.

———

A third and related ego desire is for self-esteem—the desire to feel good about ourselves and to be valued by others. This is a very dangerous desire because we all have flaws and failures. Our feeling about ourselves is interwoven with our expectations and our happiness projects and is just as vulnerable to disappointment.

Everyone wants to feel good about themselves. But self-esteem is like happiness. If it is conditional, it can be undermined by conditions. If we depend upon the fulfillment of our desires for our self-esteem, then any anticipated, imagined, or experienced failure will bring us disappointment in ourselves. Low self-esteem is disappointment with one's self, a feeling of shame. Self-esteem is a form of pride. The Tibetans distinguish "true pride" from "false pride" and "true shame" from "false shame." True pride is a sense of satisfaction with one's self for an actual accomplishment, or virtue. The pianist takes true pride in a concert well played. False pride is an exaggerated sense of self-worth without a basis in actual accomplishment—a kind of grandiosity. True shame is humble remorse for having committed a genuinely offensive or destructive act. False shame is an exaggerated sense of worthlessness which is the result of failed false pride.

If we depend on other people for our self-regard, then when we are ignored, rejected, put down, mocked, disliked, or bullied we may feel worthless. A person who feels worthless at the hands of others may become angry, aggressive, or violent. The anger conveys a feeling of self-power which is actually a pseudo-power because it a reaction to a feeling of negation, smallness, and powerlessness. A pithy Zen proverb captures the logic of the dialectic self: "People who feel small make themselves feel bigger by chopping off heads of others." This is the hidden logic of the terrorist, the assassin, and the avenger. It is also the hidden logic behind our own attempts to devalue others, to make ourselves feel larger and more powerful by diminishing the worth and effectiveness of others. We all want to be heroes in our own story. To the extent that we wish others to acknowledge and feed our narcissism, we are bound to suffer disappointment, and to turn both inwards and outwards in rage.

A couple consulted me for problems in their relationship. They were fighting and angry with each other too often. In the most recent conflict, the wife told me, she had asked her husband if he could pick up the children from school at four o'clock rather than five. He'd exploded at her. I asked him why he'd gotten angry. He answered: "I wanted to be able to help but I couldn't. We had agreed on five o'clock. I couldn't get there before then. Hey, look. I want to help. I want to be a good guy. She asked me to do something I couldn't do. I felt bad. She shouldn't have changed the plan." He was angry with his wife because she frustrated his desire to be a "good guy."

If we are to be honest, if we have any respect for the evidence, we must admit that our sense of ourselves is actually vague, delicate, and flimsy. What is self? If a biologist studies the motion of animals he will believe that the sense of self lies in motion of one form or another. If she studies genetics and neurophysiology, the self must reside in the brain. If he is a cognitive psychologist, he thinks the self lies in thought. If she is a deconstructionist, she will believe the self is a linguistic construction, a reflexive fiction written in the language of self-reference. Self is a reflection in a hall of mirrors. If we look for the source of the reflection, we shall find that there is "no *there* there."

Our sense of self is constructed. The task of growing up is to construct a sense of self and a presentation of self which are conducive to happiness. Perhaps the best way to describe the "self" is as a "bricolage." A bricolage is a patchwork of collected items pieced together into a pattern. Our sense of self is like this. It is partially based on facts: our unique face and body, our date of birth, our family tree, our ethnic identity, our occupation, and our personal history, our "resume." Other aspects of our sense of self are purely imaginary constructions: self-stories composed of memories, wishful thinking, idealized images, identification with objects, symbols and persons, judgments, expectations, hopes, false perceptions, and beliefs.

The feeling of self-continuity is created by our connecting the pieces. If we examine our actual experience of self, we discover that the connections are not stable and static, but fluctuating. Some connections become fixed and habitual, and the factual and the imaginary attach to one another and form the illusion of a coherent sense of self. If this coherence is contradicted or threatened by others, or by events, our desire to feel good about ourselves may be frustrated. *The frustration of the desire to construct and preserve a solid sense of self is the source of the most fanatical human violence and of the everyday anger that all of us suffer.*

The following story is a composite of actual events that I encounter from patients in therapy and news stories. Al was very happy with his new, red BMW. He shined it and polished it, and kept it well oiled and tuned. He was proud to own such a beautiful automobile. He felt on top of the world when he was driving around town in the leather upholstered music-hall cockpit of his shining red car. He had a very intimate relationship with his car. It was like a love affair. The car made him feel like a valid, important person. The solidity of the car gave him a solid sense of himself. Its power gave him a sense of power. This beautiful object was his and that made *him* a beautiful object. The car fulfilled his real happiness project–to feel good and proud of himself. In a sense, he had "cannibalized" the car. He had internalized its qualities as aspects of his own identity.

One day, in a parking lot, a man accidentally scraped the side of Al's car. Al became furious. It was only a little scratch, but he took it personally. He was outraged, and his adrenaline began to pump. "Why don't you watch where the hell you are going!" he shouted to the offending motorist, who was himself a man of pride who rankled at being addressed so disrespectfully. He knew he had scratched Al's car, but it was an accident. With rising energy in defense of himself he angrily replied: "It was an accident! What's wrong with you? Haven't you ever had an accident?"

To Al, the scratch on his car was an assault on his sense of self, a loss of his self-value. To the motorist, being disrespected and put down by another man threatened his proud sense of manhood. He felt foolish for being so careless, but was not going to have it shoved in his face. Each depended for their happiness on a sense of false pride.

They confronted each other like male gorillas competing to be alpha. It was a struggle for the survival of self. Al moved face to face with the motorist and stared him down: "What are you, blind? Didn't you see my car? Can't you drive, you asshole?" The motorist was bigger than Al and began to puff up. No one would call him an asshole! "You're the asshole, buddy," he shouted, and impulsively pushed Al in the chest. Al swung and missed. The motorist swung back and hit Al in the jaw. He fell. In his rage, he pulled a knife from his pocket and, with a lunge, plunged it into the motorist's stomach. The motorist died. Al was sentenced to prison for manslaughter. This may seem like an extreme illustration, but how many of us have stormed out of a job because our self-image was threatened, only to face unpaid bills? How many of us have ruined a longed-for holiday because we felt neglected or thwarted, or hurt by a loved one who failed to reinforce some treasured aspect of our sense of self?

When our desires are obstructed, the unwanted intrudes, or our sense of self is violated, we feel frustrated. What is frustration? *Frustration is the feeling of a desire combined with a perceived obstacle to its satisfaction.* Metaphorically speaking, the obstructed energy of desire is like a pent-up energy, a caged animal trying to find a way out. It is experienced as a tension, a pressure, a force meeting resistance. The degree of frustration varies with the intensity of the desire and the ability of the individual to tolerate it. Some desires are whimsical and transient. Others are intense and obsessive. We may call very strong desires "needs," but this is a rhetorical maneuver to equate wishes with survival needs like food and water. We get frustrated when we don't get what we want and intensely distressed when we don't get what we think we "need."

Many factors influence our ability to tolerate frustration: temperament and other inherited factors, early and/or overwhelming emotional traumas, training in frustration tolerance, and self-discipline, or the lack of it. The hallmark of the mature, civilized person is moderation in desire, the ability to tolerate frustration, and some sense of acceptance and contentment, even in adversity. This means accepting one's successes and failures, one's virtues and flaws with a sense of equanimity. Instead of struggling to enhance our self-esteem, which is false pride, we should remember the Zen teaching: "The wise person is of like mind in success and failure." Unfortunately, this wisdom is heresy in a competitive society, such as ours, in which self-esteem depends upon success.

The feeling of frustration has several subtle elements. It is necessary to be aware of them if we are to transform the energy of anger. The most important element is a feeling of helplessness. When we *can't* get what we want or avoid what we don't want, we feel helpless. This is the operational definition of helplessness. The moment before we explode into anger we suffer a flash of helpless feelings which are so quickly extinguished by the powerful energy of anger that most people don't notice it. People hate to feel helpless. When people are angry they often don't recognize the feeling of helplessness or will deny that they feel it. If, for some reason, anger is inhibited, the person is likely to feel helpless and cry. This is why some women, who have been trained more stringently than men to tolerate helplessness without aggression during their socialization, cry when they are angry. *The feeling of helplessness is the perceived inability to satisfy our desires: if there is no desire, there is no feeling of helplessness.*

Return to the thought experiment of a memory of being angry. Try to identify the feelings of frustration and helplessness. There was something in that situation that you felt unable to get, or to avoid. You felt a loss of control. Can you see this? Can you identify your feeling of helplessness and its relation to the anger that arises from it? One of the most important facts to remember about anger is that *the angry person feels helpless.* To the angry person, the frustrating obstacle, whether it is a person, a social entity, or a natural event, is more powerful than he is.

When we are angry we are denying and repressing our feelings of helplessness and asserting the opposite—a sense of power. Rage can look and feel powerful. It has flash and boom that can distract us from the feelings underlying it. But anger is a pseudo-power because it is born in feelings of helplessness and is motivated by the desire to deny these feelings. If we are to manage the energy of anger, we must be willing to open to them. See if you can relax your muscles, settle back into the scene you are revisiting in your thought experiment, and open to the feeling of helplessness beneath your anger. It's not easy because when we feel helpless, we usually also feel anxious. Nevertheless, try to muster the courage to open to this feeling.

The helplessness associated with a *specific* frustrated desire tends to expand into a *generalized* feeling of helplessness and vulnerability. We think that if we cannot satisfy a strong desire, it means that life could spin out of control at any moment. If the train is late and we cannot make an important appointment on time, everything could fall apart. The feelings of helplessness and vulnerability are experienced as an immediate threat to life and well-being. This feeling of being threatened resonates with the inchoate feeling of organismic vulnerability—a sense that life is dangerous, that we are helpless creatures who did not ask to be born, who cannot prevent our ultimate death, and who must yield to the vicissitudes and uncertainties of existence. This sense of danger stimulates the fight-flight reaction, which drives both the physiology and the subjective experience of anger.

It's important to understand the biology of the fight-flight response in order to fully grasp the physiological substrate of the emotions the angry person experiences. The fight-flight response is built into the animal body and is activated by the perception of danger. It prepares the body to fight or flee from present physical danger. When the organism perceives itself to be in danger, the hypothalamus and pituitary glands are alerted and, by means of nervous and hormonal messages, activate the sympathetic nervous system and adrenal glands, which prepare the body for action.

Fighting or fleeing from danger requires muscular activity. The heart beats faster and stronger, pumping nutrients to and carrying wastes away from the muscles. Blood pressure rises. Breathing becomes faster and deeper to draw oxygen into the blood. The metabolic rate increases. The skin sweats in order to cool the fired up body. To achieve these effects, the circulatory system shunts blood away from the intestines and internal organs and to the muscles, the heart and lungs, to the sensory organs, and to the brain, which becomes the watchdog and command center of the organism's defenses. This is why when we feel angry our heart races and pounds, we breathe deeper and faster, our bodies heat up and sweat, our muscles tense, our faces become taut and flushed, and our minds become alert and tightly sprung.

The difference between human and animal anger and aggression lies in the difference between the human mind and the animal mind. Animals are present-centered. Humans live in the present, but we also live in historical time, in the mental spheres of past and future. Animals react to present danger with the fight-flight reaction. They use their muscles to fight or flee. So do we. The difference is that we humans also react to the *perception or imagination of future danger* with the fight-flight reaction. The body cannot tell the difference. When the danger is future or imagined, the sympathetic-adrenal axis prepares the muscles for action as if the danger is real and present. But there is nothing to actually, physically fight or flee. The body grows tense, like an automobile with its engine racing in neutral.

There is much confusion about the difference between fear and anxiety and the nature of anxiety. In my view, *fear is a response to a present danger. Anxiety is a response to a perceived or imagined future danger. The physiology is the same.* The difference is in the mind.

When people experience extreme anxiety or panic they often feel that something physically catastrophic is happening. Often, they go to the emergency room fearing they are suffering from a heart attack. In such cases, too, it is helpful for people to be aware of the physiology of the fight-flight reaction. It helps them to understand their subjective experiences as a natural aspect of anxiety rather than a medical crisis. This by itself helps to reduce the panic.

Now look at Figure 1 again with your thought experiment in mind. Visualize the moment. Ask yourself again: *"What did I want that I was not getting?" "What was I getting that I did not want?" "How did I feel about myself?"* Can you identify the desire or aversion that fueled your anger? Can you feel the frustration and the accompanying sense of helplessness? Did you feel vulnerable, a feeling of being in some kind of danger? Can you sense the anxiety rising? Can you feel the heat of the fight-flight reaction in your body? Can you feel it ignite into anger?

Understanding of the dynamics of anger, aggression, and violence makes it more possible for us to reflect on our choices. We can choose to fuel our anger, make it hot, and explode. We know it is a choice because we can choose not to. The following chapters tell how to cultivate that choice.

7. Step Four: Reflection

TAKE SOME TIME to reflect on the dynamics of anger outlined in the previous chapter. Don't take my word about anything. Check everything against your own experience. Genuine knowledge is empirical. It is based upon experience, observation, and reflection, not on the word of others, regardless of their credentials. The view presented here is only a map. We must walk the territory of anger and see for ourselves. We can only transform the energy of anger if we understand it *authentically*, from our own experience and reflection.

A friend asked to borrow Mullah Nasrudin's donkey. "The donkey's not here," Nasrudin said emphatically. At that moment, the donkey brayed from just outside the back window. "I thought you said the donkey's not here," his friend irritably complained. "Who are you going to believe," Nasrudin answered, "me or the donkey?" Always believe the donkey.

By understanding anger we throw light into the darkest corners of ourselves. Anger is rooted in our deepest motivations: in the desire to live, prosper, and be happy, and in the aversion to unhappiness, suffering, and death. Confronting our anger honestly will reveal us to ourselves. If we are honest, we will become aware of our deepest, most hidden and powerful hopes and fears. We will see our selfishness and the techniques we use to build ourselves up, preserve, and expand ourselves. We may become disillusioned. The fairy tales we tell ourselves may begin to disintegrate. We may become frightened and tempted to flee back into the darkness.

"Perseverance furthers," the *I Ching* advises. Your efforts to work with your anger can transform you. Every flaw has a corresponding virtue into which it can be transformed. In this sense, our flaws have potential. They have value. Your anger has value. The pain of life has value. Buddha gained wisdom by examining his pain. Why would we seek to improve ourselves or our lives if we were satisfied with ourselves and with life as it is now, and if we believed it was going to be OK in the future? I have heard Tibetan lamas compare suffering to manure. Manure stinks. You wouldn't want a pile of it in your living room. But the farmer collects it and spreads it on his field. It makes the crops grow. Pain is a fertilizer, a catalyst. Pain is a motivation for change. The pain of anger and the desire for relief from that pain, for one's self and others, are the fertilizer that brings clarity and patience to flower.

The word "patience," as we have noted, is derived from the Greek root *pathos*, which means "suffering." *Patience is suffering without anger or aggression.* It is calm, willing endurance. Feeling helpless is a form of suffering. Being patient means accepting the helplessness and suffering that you cannot avoid. Clarity means understanding that these feelings issue from your desires and aversions, your happiness projects. Job is the paradigm of patience. God made him suffer, but he did not get angry at God. Job asked God, "Why have you made me suffer so?" God answered, "Who are you to ask me? Where were you when I laid the foundations of the universe?" Job opened to his suffering with humility and patience. As we open to our feelings of helplessness, we open to the reality of our creature vulnerability. Everyone suffers. As we open to this reality we have the opportunity to relax, to endure when we must, and to enjoy when we can.

As you reflect, you will see that all of the Seven Steps are in each individual step. As you become more aware of your anger and examine it more closely, you will come to understand its energy and dynamics better. As you come to understand your anger as a process within yourself, you will be more able to befriend it, as you may warm to someone you are coming to know. As you befriend it you will be more willing to approach it, to own it, and to tame it. Gradually, you will be able to recognize your anger and reflect upon it as it arises. This is not easy for the beginner. You must develop patience and the discipline to sit with the energy without repressing it or discharging it aggressively. The heat of anger can disable our powers of reflection and logical analysis. To begin, the best anyone can do is to reflect on anger after it has subsided. When I began to work on my anger years ago, I noticed that I became fully caught up in it, and it was sometimes days before I could think clearly about it. As I reflected upon each incident, I could see the pattern more clearly and more quickly. Instead of in days, I could see my part in it in hours. Hours became minutes until now, I can see it as it arises and, most of the time, ride it more gracefully. Don't be easily discouraged. Anger is so tangled up in our minds that unlearning it is like taking lace from a thorn bush.

After the anger has subsided, don't throw it away. Reflect on it. Visualize the situation and ask yourself the three core questions: "What did I want that I wasn't getting?" "What was I getting that I didn't want?" "Did I feel myself being negated?" Do this after a trivial irritation or squabble or after a major explosion. Continue to reflect and the energy of anger will become clear from your own authentic experience.

To transform the energy of anger you must be able to identify the *specific* desires and aversions that fuel it. As we have noted, sometimes they are obvious and other times they may be puzzling or hidden. Frustration of our sensuous desires is usually obvious. But anger at something seemingly trivial (the dog tracked mud on my clean floor) may be displaced from something important that we do not wish to acknowledge to ourselves or others ("I'm the only one who ever cleans the floor. I feel unloved and unappreciated by my family but I am too angry and afraid to say so. Instead, I get angry with the dog.").

Joanne consulted me for anxiety and depression. She had been seeing psychiatrists for many years, had been diagnosed as bipolar, and was heavily medicated. She had never been in psychotherapy. The medications were not working. She suffered from periods of depression punctuated by bouts of anxiety, sometimes bordering on panic. She was irritable with her husband and her children and felt that her anger was often unreasonable. She thought she needed an adjustment in her medications. I told her I would consider it after getting to know her better.

She had been born in Alabama thirty-eight years ago. Her father was a professor of literature at a local university there. Her mother was a housewife and a part-time piano teacher. Her sister was a schoolteacher, married with three children. She was brought up in a happy family, rich in culture. She was a good student and had studied painting, which she loved. In her first year of college, she fell in love with a classmate and they had a passionate affair. In the summer after the school year, he traveled in Europe with a friend. When he returned in the fall, he was cool towards her. They remained lovers, but he grew more distant and, eventually, had an affair with another classmate. Joanne was devastated. She became depressed, consulted a psychiatrist, and was prescribed an anti-depressant.

After a period of mourning, she discontinued the medication and began to socialize again. She was intelligent, cultured, interesting, and beautiful and had no trouble attracting men. She dated frequently and was sexually active, but never became attached to anyone. She focused on her schoolwork and her art and did well. After she graduated, she moved to Atlanta and took a job with a publishing firm. She had an active social life in Atlanta and, at a Christmas party, met a lawyer who fell in love with her at first sight and courted her sweetly. He was attractive, bright, and successful, and had a commanding presence. She fell in love with him. When Jim accepted a position at the Cornell Law School, he proposed to Joanne, and she accepted.

Their first year was idyllic. They were deeply in love, emotionally, intellectually, and erotically compatible, and delighted with their new life. She had time to think about a career and search for the right job. She had time to paint. She loved Ithaca, which has a wealth of creative people, and found a circle of convivial friends. Within the year, Joanne was pregnant and, the next winter, gave birth to a baby girl. With a baby, her life changed. She was devoted to her daughter, Marissa, and loved taking care of her. Her husband, however, who was not inclined to help with childcare or housework, felt abandoned. After she delivered, their sexual life came to a halt. Jim gradually stayed later at work and grew more distant. Six months after their child was born, a friend told Joanne that her husband was having an affair.

Joanne confronted Jim angrily. He promised to end his affair, but delayed for months. Joanne became depressed, consulted a psychiatrist, and was again placed on an anti-depressant without having the opportunity to discuss her pain and her choices. After Jim ended his affair, their marriage gradually stabilized, but with a coolness, a reservoir of cold resentment. When Marissa was three years old, and in nursery school several days a week, Joanne met a man at a luncheon with friends and began an affair with him. After several months, she confessed to Jim. He was angry but, compromised by his own indiscretion, he forgave Joanne. They decided to renew their commitment by having another child, and then another.

When Joanne came to see me, Marissa was fourteen, her son was ten, and the youngest was an eight-year-old girl. She loved her children and spent a lot of time with them, but she complained that her life was taken up by childcare and housework, which she hated. She had no time to paint, no time to exercise, and little time to see her friends. Jim had a successful career, expected to come home to a neat house and a cooked dinner, and was sexually demanding. She confessed that she was still angry with Jim about his affair. She was even more angry with him because he forbade her to go into town alone out of fear that she would have another affair. She felt consumed by him and resented his sexual demands. She felt negated by his commanding presence and dominating air.

As we talked in our sessions, I focused on Joanne's anger. She was often irritable with Jim and sometimes with her children, about which she felt guilty. She wasn't even sure she had the right to be angry at Jim. Except for the affair, he was really a good man, they were financially comfortable, they lived in a charming house, and were, by all outward signs, a happy family. But Joanne was miserable.

I asked her, what would make her happy? What did she want and what didn't she want? Reflecting on these questions helps to transform anger into clarity. It raises self-examination to the level of one's relation to life as a whole. Her instantaneous, almost snarled response was that she wasn't sure she wanted to be married to Jim. She had thought about having another affair. Over the next few sessions, I encouraged her to consider her choices. Divorce was a choice. Having an affair was a choice. Working with her marriage was also a choice. As she thought about it, and reflected on the horrors of divorce, single parenthood, and the changes they would bring, she realized she would have even more work and less time. As she thought about having an affair, she guessed that if she did Jim also would and they would end in divorce anyway. Unhappy as she was with her life, she decided to stick with it and work with it.

Reflecting on her anger, she realized that there were givens in her life, some of which she could not change and some of which she did not want to change. She could not change the past. She could not undo the affairs. She was approaching middle age. She was married. And she had three children, whom she loved, and whose lives and home she had to manage. She could not make Jim into a different person. She loved him but she was angry and uncomfortable with him.

She realized that she also had choices. Having rejected the option of divorce, the obvious choice, then, was to work with Jim, to be honest with him about her feelings, to ask him for what she wanted and what she could do for him. Over the course of the next month, she had several talks with Jim about their relationship and her life. To her relief, Jim was very receptive. He affirmed his love for her and his commitment to their marriage. They both agreed that having an affair was not a constructive option. She talked frankly with him about their sexual differences. She had little interest in sex, partly because of her resentment, which distanced her from her husband, and partly as the result of the anti-depressants she was on. He was highly sexually charged, very attracted to her, and very frustrated.

Confronting their sexual problem required both of them to reflect on the principle of balance—in this case, balance between what each could get and what each would give, the balance between self-interest and compassion. As she reflected, Joanne realized that she had a right to reject sex and that Jim had the right to want it, and that if they both insisted on their rights they would be incompatible. For their marriage to survive, they each had to surrender something to the other. Fortunately, Jim was understanding and agreed to moderate his sexual demands and to respect her feelings. She reciprocated by determining to take more of an interest in sex, which she had always enjoyed. She realized that although she was not necessarily instantly aroused when he caressed her, she could warm to the experience and enjoy it. To facilitate this, we cautiously and gradually reduced the dose of her anti-depressant.

As Joanne and Jim continued to work on their relationship, her anger and irritability waned and she was more appreciative of his efforts and devotion. Nevertheless, she continued to experience bouts of anxiety and generalized irritability. I asked her again to examine her anger. What did she want and what did she not want? As we reflected, Joanne reiterated that she still felt constricted and suffocated by childcare and housework. She had no time to paint, no time for friends, and barely time for exercise and yoga, to which she was devoted. As we inquired more deeply, it became apparent that Joanne had two contradictory desires. On the one hand, she had accepted the fact that she was married. She loved her children and wanted to care for them. On the other hand, she felt suffocated by her obligations. She wanted to be free, to have a life, to pursue her own interests. Neither desire could be completely satisfied, which frustrated her, and her frustration made her feel helpless, anxious, and irritable.

As she reflected on her anger and her contradictory desires, Joanne could see herself, her life, and her predicament from a broader perspective. She could not have everything she wanted. If she wanted to care for her children and to live in an orderly house, she could not also be free of them. Up until now, she had resented her obligations and felt guilty when she took time for herself. She was anxious when she abandoned her duties to her children, angry when she performed them, and depressed because she had lost the hope of ever finding a happy solution to her dilemma.

I suggested that since she had decided not to leave her children and her home, she might take responsibility for her choice and do it as a dance rather than as a burden. We also discussed ways in which she could find the time to do what she loved. She had a room in the house in which she could paint, but she had been so lost in her anger and self-pity that she had not set it up. With a little effort, she could start a painting and work at it in her free time. She agreed that she would have more time for herself if she managed her life better and had a little support from her husband.

Once she understood her anger and reflected on her life, Joanne was better able to accept the givens of her situation, conditions that she could not or was not willing to change. She was better able to make choices where she could to bring herself into balance. Her feelings of anxiety, anger, and depression subsided, although she was an emotionally expressive person and continued to experience a full range of manageable feelings. As she reflected, she could see her life in the perspective of time. She could see the continuities and changes through the stages of her life. She could see how past choices had unintended and unimagined consequences which became the realities of her present life. She realized that she could learn to work with the limitations and opportunities presented by those realities. She could choose a positive attitude within the range of her choices, rather than lamenting what she could not have and could not be.

Reflect on your thought experiment. After identifying and reflecting upon the desires which fueled your anger, try to identify the obstruction to the satisfaction of those desires. What stopped you from getting what you wanted or avoiding what you didn't want? The obstacles may be outside or within yourself. Someone else might have been better qualified than you for the job you wanted and were denied. Or you may have lost it because of your own ambivalence about taking it. You may face an insuperable obstacle. Or you may expect too much.

Can you think of another way you might have handled the situation? Could you have gotten what you wanted, or avoided the unwanted, by saying or doing something different? Sometimes we get in our own way. Try to imagine the other person's point of view. Reflect on how this situation fit or didn't fit with your happiness projects.

Focus your attention on the cascade of feelings associated with frustration. Go slowly here. First, identify the feeling of helplessness. Don't rush through it. Learn to sit with it. Paradoxical as it may sound, learning to sit with the feeling of helplessness is empowering. You may not have power over the external situation, but you have power over yourself.

Can you see how your feelings of helplessness become generalized into a feeling of vulnerability? Reflect on the fact that your power to control your life is limited. No one can control the course of history, or the economy, or other people. Most of us can barely control ourselves. Can you accept the fact that you may not get everything you want or be able to avoid everything you dislike or fear? See for yourself how the feeling of vulnerability makes you anxious. We can anticipate or imagine problems as if they are happening now. "What if I don't have enough money to retire?" "What if I lose my job?" "What if my sick baby dies?" The body cannot tell the difference between real and imagined danger. It reacts to both with fight or flight. When we cannot sit with the energy of desire and helplessness, the energy of the fight-flight reaction fuels our anger and aggression.

Reflecting on our anger unlocks the deepest secrets of our minds and hearts. Remember the big picture. You are witnessing a powerful biological response to a sense of creature vulnerability. The energy of anger is the energy of desire, which is the energy of life. Frustration is a feeling that there is some obstacle to the life force. The feelings of helplessness and vulnerability are experienced as a threat to life and the integrity of self. Anxiety is a feeling of future danger to self and its happiness projects. Anger is a natural biological response to the perception of danger.

Reflecting on our anger takes us directly to desires and aversions that we cherish and cling to but may be only dimly aware of and unwilling to take responsibility for. It helps us to understand our feelings. Frustration becomes easier to bear as we become more open to our feelings of helplessness. Anxiety is more likely to subside when we realize that the future danger is either unavoidable or manageable. Our commitment to working with our anger strengthens as we see its destructive consequences. The redeeming irony of anger is that, even when nothing can be done for us to have our way, we still have the choice to resist the fact or to accept it. There are some things we have no choice about. But we have the choice of how to respond to the limitations on our choice. We have the choice to fight the feeling of helplessness or to relax into it.

As we reflect and remember that we are both individuals and representatives of a species, we can develop some kindness and compassion for ourselves. We are poor, confused humans trying to find our way. At the same time, we can better understand the anger, aggression, and violence of others. They too are human. We are all pursuing happiness by trying to get what we want, to avoid what we don't want, and to maintain a sense of self-respect. To understand anger, aggression, and violence is not to ignore its bitter fruits or to excuse it. Instead, understanding helps us to get past our own feelings of hatred and the desire for revenge, which only breed more chaos. If we are to renounce violence and negotiate our conflicts, then we must all be willing to also renounce some of our desires and to accept some things we would rather not. The fruit of reflection is compassion, for ourselves and for others.

8. Step Five: Decision

HAVING REFLECTED upon the dynamics of anger, aggression, and violence, and checked them against your own experience, it is time to affirm a commitment, make an assessment, and come to a decision. At first, as we are becoming familiar with this step, we will consider these actions one at a time. Eventually, we apply them together on the spot as anger arises.

The commitment is the renewed intention to take responsibility for your anger rather than blaming others, and to experience it fully rather than repressing it or acting it out destructively. This commitment must be actively renewed every time anger arises. If you do not renew it regularly, you will likely fall back into the tendency to blame others and to explode in anger. This commitment is not easy. It requires paying attention, establishing a clear intention, and exercising self-control. It is a matter of self-discipline.

The assessment involves an evaluation of the situation to see if there is some way you can get what you want, avoid what you don't want, or ameliorate the pain of your bruised ego. There is nothing wrong with feeling good about yourself if no one is harmed. The purpose of life is to enjoy it. The basic ethical rule is "Do no harm"—to yourself or others. The question is: "Can you get what you want and avoid what you don't want, or accept some compromise without harming yourself or others?"

The answers require both a practical (can I?) and a moral (should I?) assessment. The practical assessment addresses the question: "Can you find a way around, over, or through the obstacles which are frustrating your desires?" This may or may not be possible. As you assess the situation, keep an open mind to the possibility that you may not get what you want—in fact, you may get what you don't want. This thought will help you to rein in the demanding energy of your desire as you assess the practical options. Keep a positive attitude. Don't rely on the hope or expectation that your wish will be fulfilled for your positive attitude. Stay positive as a policy, not as a barometer. Stay present and aware as you relate openly to the situation. Keep in mind that overcoming obstacles may be difficult and painful, and may take time and effort. It may require great patience, perseverance, flexibility, imagination, and an openness to that which you cannot control.

Sometimes, you have to make a choice on the spot. For instance, if a waiter accidentally spills soup on your suit, you would have several choices. You could become angry and assault him, and face criminal charges. You could storm out of the restaurant and brood for a week about your ruined evening and the carelessness of other people. You could take a rather theatrical moral high road and graciously forgive the accident with the stipulation that the restaurant pay for the dry cleaning and forget the check. That might satisfy your sense of justice and allow you to feel like a fair but firm fellow.

Or, you could simply forgive the waiter and bear the burden yourself. It was an accident. He didn't mean to spill the soup on your pants. No doubt, he hides his guilt and apprehension behind his sincere apologies. He would be happy if you forgave him. Perhaps he would think of you as a kind and wonderful person. On the other hand, you would have to pay for your own dry cleaning, and the meal. You might have to let go of your desire for justice. You might have to let go of your pride and even your dignity, since you would have to finish your dinner with wet pants. Somehow, running through all the fundamentally egotistical options can trip one's sense of humor and proportion. You could decide to take the whole situation quite lightly, as a humorous mishap with no truly dire consequences. You might have a perfectly pleasant, if slightly moist, evening.

Which would you choose? You may not yet have realized that anger is a choice, because until now you may not have known about or reasonably considered the possibility. But now that you know that there *are* other options, you cannot escape the fact that anger is a choice. Aggression is a choice. Violence is a choice. It's up to you. The Greek philosopher, Epictetus, advises: "First decide what manner of man you want to be. When you have settled this, act upon it in all you do."

The practical assessment will determine what options you have and which strategies you might pursue. The moral assessment will determine what kind of person you are and want to be. You as a person are responsible for your anger. How you respond to your anger will not only display, but also determine, your character.

There is a lot of confusion about the definitions of and the difference between character and personality. "Personality" is all that a person reveals about himself through word, emotional expression, and deed. We say that a man has a sparkling personality if he is entertaining, tells interesting stories, is positive, and has a winning smile and a sense of humor. We say a man has a dark personality if he is emotionally intense, negative, and depressed, or cynical about life.

Character is the moral aspect of personality. It is a measure of how a person manages his or her desires, aversions, and self-interest. We say a man has character if he endures travail with grace, equanimity, good humor, and patience. Patience, as we have noted, is suffering without aggression. This means suffering the frustration of not having what you want without anger. It means gracefully enduring what you don't want or don't like without anger. It means developing humility and self-control, flexibility and proportion, rather than egotistic self-indulgence. These are the measures of character. A person can have a fascinating personality and bad character, and vice versa.

This view of character suggests a spectrum of character types with two extreme poles and a middle ground. At one pole are persons who indulge their desires and aversions heedlessly with little regard for the consequences. Their selfishness is often offensive and creates problems for themselves and others. Because of the tendency to medicalize moral issues, these persons are often "diagnosed" as mentally ill with such labels as "psychopath," "sociopath," "antisocial personality," "borderline personality," and now, increasingly, "bipolar disorder." The idea that their behavior is a moral problem is not usually considered.

At the other pole are persons who renounce their desires, who open to or even invite pain, and who negate and subordinate themselves. The serene, ascetical monk may sincerely renounce the world in the belief that it is for the benefit of all sentient beings and his own salvation. Many ascetics have difficulty renouncing the egotistical desire to think of themselves, and to be thought of by others, as good people because they are unselfish. Some people benefit from their martyrdom, ostentatiously serving others before themselves, often with a display of pain that creates gratitude and sometimes guilt in their beneficiaries. The suicide martyr renounces life itself, ostensibly in the service of others, but with the expectation of divine praise and immortality. Those who renounce their desires are often admired, while those who indulge them are usually denounced.

Most of us live in the middle ground, indulging where we can and renouncing where we must, constantly faced with the moral decision of what to do and how to do it. Most of our decisions are easy and we don't think of them as moral choices. Nevertheless, we attach some "good" to whatever we choose, even between coffee and tea. Some choices are trivial and inconsequential. Others are heavy with meaning and consequence and become moral questions and prescriptions. In these cases, it is clear that choice is the essence of morality.

The issues of ethics, morality, and character arise when our choices are obstructed by others, judged by others, or affect others.

What if you can only get what you want through intimidation, manipulation, cheating, or other immoral or illegal means? You might get away with it. But you have harmed someone and that person may want revenge. A thief may get momentary satisfaction from a successful robbery, but the chances are he will eventually go to prison. Even if he is never caught, he will always be looking over his shoulder. If we use our friends for our own selfish purposes, if we manipulate or coerce others into doing our will, if we always think "me first" and get angry when someone else prevails, we are bound for trouble and unhappiness. The imperative of self is to do for one's self. The imperative of social ethics is to do for others. Choosing between these two paths is what it means to be a moral animal!

Society imposes legal, moral, and conventional limitations on the satisfaction of our desires. The fact that we are social animals and must live in harmony with others requires limits on our options and actions. This generates frustration in all of us because we can't have everything we want and must endure some things we don't want, and it creates guilt because we still harbor our most passionate prohibited desires and aversions. When, as often happens, we cannot find a satisfactory moral or legal way to satisfy our strong and insistent desires, when we feel that there is nothing we can say or do to ameliorate our pain and humiliation, we are vulnerable to frustration, helplessness, anxiety, anger, and depression.

After renewing your commitment to work with your anger and assessing the practical and moral means to satisfy your desires, the next step is making a decision. It is important to remember that *resolving anger requires making a conscious decision.* The energy of anger is the energy of a frustrated desire. If you cannot find a way to satisfy a strong desire and if you do not recognize and accept that the desire cannot be satisfied, your anger will gain momentum. *Making a decision drains anger of its energy.*

As we assess the options available to overcome the obstacles to the satisfaction of our desires, we need to think of creative responses and muster the courage to act on them. I am not talking here about macho courage, about bulling or bullying through discomfort, which is the coward's way, motivated by fear and pride. I am talking about spiritual courage. Perhaps the choice most likely to succeed requires patience, diplomacy, a humble apology, or a temporary defeat. Accepting defeat requires a great deal of courage, but it could turn out to be a victory if you have avoided the negative consequences of your anger. Sometimes the best choice is to do nothing and work with the pain.

Sandra was a fifty-three-year-old woman who consulted me for depression. Five years ago, she was told by her family doctor that she was suffering from clinical depression caused by a biochemical imbalance. He placed her on Prozac. No further inquiries were made into her life or feelings. After six months, with no improvement, her doctor switched her to Paxil, and then, over time, to Zoloft and then to Celexa, all without success. She had recently moved to Ithaca and needed a psychiatrist to prescribe and regulate her medication.

I told Sandra, as I tell all my patients, that before I prescribe a drug I want to know more about her. I asked her to tell me about herself: "Give me a thumbnail autobiography." She was born in a small town near Buffalo, New York into a Fundamentalist Christian family. Her father was a retired minister. Her mother died when she was twelve years old. She had an older sister and an older brother. As her father grew older and her siblings left home, responsibility for his care fell on Sandra.

Wanting to be a good person, a good daughter, and a good Christian, Sandra devoted herself to her father's care. She graduated from a local college and took a master's degree in education. For years, she taught at a local elementary school and lived at home with her father. Periodically, she would become depressed and seek psychotherapy, with temporary relief. Her last therapist suggested she take an anti-depressant. Two years ago, she met a man in church who lived in Ithaca and was visiting relatives in Buffalo. They were instantly attracted to each other. He courted her and they quickly fell in love. After six months, he proposed. After painful deliberation with great guilt about leaving her father, she accepted his proposal and moved to Ithaca to join him a year ago.

I asked about her marriage. She praised her husband effusively. He was kind, gentle, considerate, unflappable, and patient with her. Her marriage was fine, she said. She had found a job teaching at a local elementary school, which she loved. She had made friends in Ithaca and had a satisfying social life. "And what about your father?" I asked. She told me that although he suffered from painful severe arthritis he could manage his house and needed help only with shopping. She visited him in Buffalo as often as she could, twice a month at a minimum, and helped him to shop and do chores he was unable to manage. Her brother and her sister lived near him, but they complained that they were too busy with their families and work to help very much.

As she talked about her father, I could see that she was angry. I could tell from her tone of voice, her facial expression, and her body tension. As I have said, anger often accompanies or lies beneath depression. It's not quite right to say that her depression was masking her anger. It was a transformation of it. Depression is not anger turned inward, as many people believe. The dynamics of anger and depression are the same up to a point. Both anger and depression are the result of frustrated desires or dashed hopes. Both the angry person and the depressed person feel helpless. Anger requires hope, the hope that, somehow, aggression will yield fruit. When hope is lost, depression sets in. Depression is anger without passion, without power, and without hope. Sandra was angry without the passion, without the energy. She was frustrated and angry but had given up hope.

"What are you angry about?" I asked, somewhat spontaneously. At first, she was surprised that I thought she was angry, and she angrily denied it. Gradually, as she talked about her father, it became obvious to her that she was angry. As she opened to her anger, her depression began to lift, as often happens. She still felt helpless, but the awareness of her anger revived her hopes because it meant that she had a choice.

She was extremely exasperated by her father, who was very authoritarian and demanding. Her mother had treated her father like a king. For years after her mother died she had lived with her imperious father, serving him faithfully, complying with his every whim. She didn't go out socially like her friends did. She avoided men, feeling that if she married she would be abandoning her father. Yet she yearned for a life of her own. When she met Harry and fell in love, she yielded to her desires and, although she felt a strong undercurrent of guilt, she married him and moved away.

Her father continued to make demands on her, however. He called often, complaining with subtle indignation that she was neglecting him. He frequently asked Sandra to take him shopping, to take him to the doctor, to help him with house chores that he was unable to do. Sandra fell into the habit of being on call for her father and visiting him at least twice a month to shop for him and clean his house. She was angry at him and felt guilty about feeling angry. She condemned herself for being selfish. After all, he was eighty-five years old and was increasingly handicapped by arthritis. She was also angry at her brother and sister who, she felt, neglected their father and selfishly pursued their own lives. Every time she was about to visit her father or when she returned from a visit, she was filled with rage and didn't know why.

I encouraged her to take responsibility for her anger and to examine it. What did she want that she was not getting? What was she getting that she didn't want? After many months of reflection, she began to realize that she wanted many things. Firstly, she wanted to be and feel like a good person. This desire obligated her to yield to her father's wishes lest she be vulnerable to feeling guilty for abandoning him. Secondly, she didn't want to be on call to respond to his every demand. She had difficulty facing this desire because it contradicted her desire to be a good person. Thirdly, she wished her father was a different person. She wished he was more self-reliant and less demanding. She also wished he would show more appreciation for what she was doing rather than taking it for granted as his entitlement. Fourthly, she wanted her brother and sister to help their father more so she could be relieved of compulsory travel to Buffalo. Finally, she wanted other people to sacrifice their own selfish desires for the sake of others, as she had done. These frustrated desires made her angry at almost everyone in her family.

The root cause of her anger was her guilt. We often don't recognize how resentment is the bitter fruit of guilt. We think of guilt as a form of regret and self-condemnation for an anti-social or illegal act, or wish. Most people feel guilty when they know they have done something wrong, such as breaking a law or violating an ethical principle. This form of guilt is just the tip of the iceberg.

Guilt is social cement. As Freud understood, guilt is a byproduct of civilization, which requires the renunciation of certain strongly held desires for the sake of belonging to the group. Indulging in forbidden desires generates guilt. Clinging to these desires even without indulging them also generates guilt. Relationships require the renunciation of some desires. In every relationship, boundaries and rules are established which require each person to renounce a degree of freedom in order to preserve the bond. If the boundaries or the rules are violated, the bond is threatened.

In marriage, for example, couples agree to be sexually monogamous. If one of them has an extra-marital affair, the marriage is threatened. Guilt is a restriction on freedom. It functions to repress and control desires which, if pursued, might result in one's being socially rejected or losing a relationship to which one is attached. It's not necessary do something wrong to feel guilty—only to harbor the wish. As a result, the guilty person resents the person whom they blame for their loss of freedom. Sandra grew up with the rule that she was obligated to take care of her father. She experienced this as a restriction on her freedom and, without being aware of it, she resented him for it.

The resolution of guilt requires making a free choice. One must either consciously and voluntarily indulge the desire or renounce it, one or the other. Ambivalence breeds guilt. I invited Sandra to explore her possible choices. She could decide not to travel to Buffalo for her father's sake at all and to leave his care to her siblings who lived closer to him. Or, she could choose to serve him sometimes but not always. She could talk to her siblings again and ask for them to do more. Or, she could decide of her own free will to continue what she was doing.

We agreed that it would be difficult for her to simply abandon her father. She loved him and felt sorry that he was in pain and handicapped. She wanted to help him. On the other hand, the present arrangement was not acceptable. She felt exploited by him and by her siblings. I asked if she had talked to her brother and sister about sharing responsibility for their father's care. She said she had, but they complained that he lived on the other side of town, that they had their own families, and they were working full-time jobs. "Well," I said, "you live four hours away, you now have your own family, and you are working full-time. Perhaps you can talk to them again?"

Sandra responded negatively with angry, cynical complaints about her brother. He is a man and men aren't expected to care for their parents. Boys are treated differently than girls. When she was young, her brother was free to do what he wanted while she was protected and restricted by her father. Her brother wouldn't help around the house. He would say that he was busy with his work. Her sister liked to travel and often found it inconvenient to respond to her father's needs. She was afraid to confront them because she was sure they would reject her pleas and would criticize her for abandoning her father. She could not stand the idea that others might see her as selfish.

I explained to her that her anger was the product of her conflicting desires and fears. She loved her father and wanted to help him. She wanted to feel like and be seen as a good person. She didn't want to travel to Buffalo so often but was afraid she would be criticized and rejected by her family if she didn't. If she could address this conflict, perhaps she could see the situation differently and resolve her anger.

Resolving her anger required getting clear about what was in her power to change and what she could not change, and making decisions about what she was willing to change and what she was not willing to change. She could not change her father. He was elderly and his character and style were fixed. Besides, he was a stubborn patriarch. She could not expect that he could do more for himself. Her father was who he was. She was the youngest and the burden had fallen on her by default. She had accepted it. She could make choices now, but she could not change the past. She also could not control other people's opinion of her. People are free to think what they will. If she continued to serve her father obediently, some people might think she was a saint and others that she was a sap. If she tried to persuade her brother and sister to help, some people might think she was dodging her responsibilities, while others might think she was courageously seeking fairness.

Sandra could see that she resented her feelings of obligation because they required her to sacrifice her freedom. She did not feel she could freely choose not to respond to her father's needs. She resented her siblings who acted selfishly, without the guilt that she felt. She could not both serve her father and be free of him. Wanting what she could not have frustrated her and made her angry. It took her a while to reflect on this and to accept it. She decided to call her brother and sister again and ask for their help. Gradually, as they negotiated, they yielded to her pleas and agreed to do more.

At first, she was relieved. She felt she had been heard. She did not feel condemned for abandoning her father. Nevertheless, she still became irritated when he called and asked for help. She still became angry when her brother or sister made excuses for not being available to help on specific occasions. She felt they had agreed to relieve her of some of the responsibility but still acted as if it was primarily hers. She continued to feel guilty when she told her father that it was her brother's or sister's turn to help and not hers. She still felt that she was abandoning her father and imposing on her siblings.

But she examined her irritation and confirmed for herself that she still harbored impossible wishes. Gradually, she began to accept the situation as is. She did not want to abandon her father, but she also did not want to be angry with him when he asked for help. The solution was to make choices without feeling she was forced out of obligation and guilt. She developed the willingness to sometimes say no and she got some of what she wanted, but not all. She was happy that her siblings had agreed to help more and, in the future, might be persuaded to help more equitably. The realization that she could make choices raised her hopes and relieved her depression.

Sandra could make an empowering decision because she directly faced the questions: "What do I want that I am not getting?" "What am I getting that I don't want?" "Is there a way I can get what I want?" "Am I willing to accept half a loaf?" Instead of feeling obligated and guilty, she took responsibility for her choices. Her actions didn't change much. She still went to Buffalo every few months. But her feeling about it changed, and her anger subsided.

The best guidance in answering these questions is expressed in the Serenity Prayer: "Grant me the serenity to accept the things I cannot change, courage to change the things I can, and the wisdom to know the difference." If we have the insight and moral fiber to find an ethical way to satisfy our desires, then we need the courage to pursue that course. It often happens, however, that we cannot immediately think of ways to get what we want or to avoid what we don't want. There may be nothing we can do or say to relieve our feelings of frustration. How can we achieve serenity when we are feeling frustrated, helpless, vulnerable, and anxious?

9. Step Six: Relaxing and Letting Go

SERENITY IS DIFFICULT enough to achieve when things are going our way. It is a heroic task to remain serene while pursuing our endless desires and happiness projects as well as struggling to avoid unavoidable pain. It takes courage to stay calm and hopeful in the face of bewilderment about life and the knowledge of certain death. It's a real challenge to remain serene when things are going wrong.

Modern people have become intoxicated by the idea of progress, which is a very new idea in human history. It is only as old as modern science, about three hundred years. Before that, history was conceived of not as upwardly linear but as circular and spiral, eternal return spiced with eternal change. The idea of progress invites us to expect that our lives will continuously improve. Sometimes, we lose hope when things merely level off, as if it is the beginning of the end.

The fact that science and technology have been constantly improving doesn't mean that our lives will continuously improve. Science and technology cannot guarantee that we will be progressively happier, or even protect us from everyday unhappiness. They will not get us to heaven or win us immortality. Where desire arises, so do obstacles. Desire and obstacle are opposite faces of the same coin. Things can go our way. They can go our way for a long time and gloriously. Eventually, however, things are bound to go wrong. The happiest life ends in old age and death. For ordinary people, things regularly go wrong, not because a malevolent force is out to get us, but because life doesn't always work out the way we want. Our expectations and hopes are out of touch with reality. This is the basis of the stress that plagues "advanced" societies.

What is stress? The question is pertinent for several reasons. First, stress is often given as an explanation, or an excuse, for anger. People get angry more easily and more often when they are under stress. Second, relaxation is widely and, in my view, correctly, regarded as an antidote to stress. If learning to relax is a key to transforming the energy of stress-generated anger, then we must understand the state of stress for which it is an antidote, for that is where we are starting from.

Basically, stress is a product of the struggle for survival. It is a reaction to a threat to life and, in humans, a threat to happiness. In highly complex, advanced societies, few can escape it. Sometimes it is stressful just to get up in the morning and face the day. The children must be dressed, fed, and sent off to school on time. The task is stressful because of the anxiety that if they are too often late they might fail—in school and in life. Then, we must get ourselves off to work on time. We rush for the subway or bus, dodging obstacles. Or we drive through hectic traffic dodging obstacles, nervously checking our watches. Our stomachs are tight and tense from the anxiety that, if we are late, we could be fired or demoted. We work against a background of anxiety that if we don't perform well and please the boss, our lives could fall apart. There are so many difficult people to deal with, so many rules to follow and forms to fill out, so many bills to pay. What if someone we love gets sick, or fails, or suffers, or dies? The roof must be patched or the rain will rot the house. Where will the money come from for that? And what about that vacation we yearn for so we can relax and escape all this stress? Sometimes it feels like just being alive is almost too stressful to bear.

Stress is associated with such a wide variety of conditions that the term seems to have no specific meaning. It can refer to any noxious situation, as if anything unpleasant can be stressful. It also refers to our mental and physical reactions to the external event.

The outer events "stress" us, and we are "stressed." Hans Selye, one of the first innovative thinkers on the subject, distinguished between "stressors," the outer conditions, and "stress," our reactions to them. Stress can manifest in our minds, our mental attitudes, and our energy. It can manifest in our feelings as tension and anxiety. And it can manifest in our bodies as genuine medical disease. What is this ubiquitous experience which sets up so much of our suffering and unhappiness?

The meaning of the word "stress" can be understood from its ordinary uses. Language has its archeology. As human consciousness grows more complex and subtle, the meaning of words is transformed, like a modern city built upon ancient ruins. At the most basic, physical level, stress refers to an external, applied force that strains, deforms, damages, or destroys an object. For example, a tightening vise stresses and crushes the wood in its jaws. The heat of an acetylene torch stresses and melts steel. A delicate porcelain teacup falls and shatters on the floor from the stress of the impact.

At a more abstract level, stress refers to a relative emphasis in language and music, e.g., to stress a syllable, a word, or a beat. Here, "stress" is a metaphor drawn from physical stress, as if the explosion of air which gives emphasis to the syllable or beat "distorts" the normal sound or rhythm. The ironic twist of this meaning is, that while the emphasis distorts the normal sound, it creates a new sound which is pleasing rather than destructive, suggesting that stress may have a positive as well as a negative value.

At a higher level of abstraction, stress has the psychological meaning of a traumatic experience. The term "trauma" connotes the two poles of stress: the outer, traumatic event and the inner, traumatic reaction. A popular concept of psychological stress is modeled after physical stress, of which it is a metaphor. (The mind can only be described with metaphors.) It suggests the image of an external psycho-social force, such as the loss of a job or a death in the family, that acts upon the mind and emotions, distorting and fragmenting them, like a bullet smashing into bone. This metaphor may be mistakenly interpreted to suggest that mind is a *tabula rasa*, a "blank tablet" upon which experiences are passively imprinted. However, our own reflections on anger teach us that mind is not a passive object, like a tablet. We have choices. We have, to varying degrees, the ability to respond flexibly. The mind is not blank and anergic. It is an active, organismic agent which interprets sensory input and invests it with meaning in relation to its striving for life, safety, and satisfaction.

This view actually better fits the physical paradigm of stress. The effect of a physical force on an object depends not only on the strength of the force but also on the toughness of the object. Glass is fragile. Wood is stressed more easily than steel. Diamonds are created by stress and are relatively impervious to it. Similarly, certain states of mind make us more vulnerable to or more resistant to stress than others.

People have different capacities to respond to stress, depending on many factors. Some people are experienced in handling stress and handle it well. Others crumble under it. We could name any number of causal explanations for this difference. It could depend upon a person's past stresses, how traumatic they were, or how much support they had. It could depend upon conditioning, modeling, temperament, or health. Some think that the vulnerability to stress indicates a biochemical imbalance of some vague and unspecified nature. The capacity to endure stress also depends upon an act of will. It depends upon whether one wants to persevere or to crumble. Sometimes people tell me that they are at the end of their rope. I tell them, "Give yourself more rope. There is no rope in the first place. It's just your imaginary rope." How much stress we can bear depends, to a large extent, upon how much we are willing to bear.

Some people are stressed by not having enough money to buy a new car. They take it very personally, as an assault on their pride, their sense of self. They can't tolerate the humiliation they would feel driving a rust-bucket. Where does that place them as persons on the scale of social value? Some people are stressed when they can't pay their bills on time. Some people are stressed when there are dirty dishes in the sink or the neighbors are noisy. People can be stressed by anything going wrong or, even, by the possibility that things *may* go wrong. The truth is that nothing ever goes wrong except in the mind of the person who sees it as wrong because it is not what he wishes it to be. Outside of our minds, nothing in the universe is right or wrong. It just is.

Some people are stressed because they are perfectionists. Perfectionism is an instructive phenomenon. It is like a cartoon, a hyperbole, whose exaggerated qualities suggest qualities we also possess, but more moderately. A perfectionist is a person whose mission in life is to avoid flaws or mistakes at any cost. I often see students in my office who suffer from perfectionism. They usually come because they are anxious and depressed and think they are mentally ill. Once their perfectionism is identified, the dynamics become clear. They very often procrastinate doing their schoolwork because they want it to be perfect. They want to remember perfectly and write perfectly. Because they doubt their ability to achieve this, they avoid their tasks or suffer from procrastination. As a result, they hand their work in late, their grades fall, and they become anxious and depressed about the prospect of failure. One student, a senior, came in depressed because her straight A record was spoiled by a B. Perfectionists suffer at every endeavor because their desire is impossible to achieve. No one and nothing is perfect, except in the sense that it is perfect as is.

Perfectionists constantly look for what they are trying to avoid. They are constantly looking for what they fear. All a perfectionist sees are flaws and mistakes. I had an aunt who was a perfect housekeeper. In every room she went into, she looked for dirt. She was always looking for dirt. To a perfectionist, the possibility of encountering dirt, disorder, or imperfection is stressful. It is a sign and a symptom of their creature vulnerability. If something can go wrong, everything can go wrong. Their perfectionism is a ritualistic pattern of avoiding failure, pain, sickness, and death. On the other hand, almost everyone is stressed by the possibility of failure, pain, sickness, and death. The operative words are "almost everyone."

I recall my first sight of a dead body. In my freshman year of medical school the first class was anatomy. On the first morning, the class gathered outside the dissection room. The professor let us into the room all at one time, as if the show was about to start. Twenty cadavers lay on twenty catafalques covered by oilcloth. We sat silently for a while by the side of our assigned corpse, in groups of four, waiting for the room to settle down. The professor then asked us to remove the oilcloth and inspect the body.

My cadaver had a tag with his name on it, Joseph Goldstein. He looked about seventy-five years old. Once he was alive. Now he was dead and I was going to dissect his body. I shivered. We were all stressed by the experience. After an hour of nervous inspection of a naked corpse, our wise professor dismissed the class. The experience reverberated through the day as a fascination and anxiety about death. Some wondered whether they could get through the anatomy course. Day by day, as we became involved in the dissection, our stress waned. By the end of the month we were eating lunch while we worked, resting our sandwiches on Joseph Goldstein's ankles while dissecting his intestines. The stress was gone. The situation had not changed. Our minds had. The degree of stress depends upon a quality of mind.

People are "stressed out," to one degree or another, by the fear of things gone or going wrong. This is a good definition of stress— "the fear of things being wrong, going wrong, or staying wrong." Survival and well-being—of the body and the self—are endangered by things going wrong. Notice that this definition of stress is similar to our definition of anxiety—"The fear of future or imagined danger." In my view, there is no difference between stress and anxiety. They are both responses to a perceived danger. Stress *is* anxiety and anxiety is stressful. They arise from the same state of mind and have the same physiology.

The state of mind which predisposes to stress is the same as that which predisposes to anxiety, anger, aggression, and violence. It is the "normal" state of mind, by which I mean ordinary mind, which pursues pleasure and happiness in the service of self and defends itself against pain and unhappiness. The stronger, more fervently, and more stubbornly held are the desires, hopes, and fears, the greater the vulnerability to stress.

The "normal" state of mind is attached and tense. We are attached to our happiness projects and tense about things going wrong. This is the breeding ground of stress. The increasing complexity of modern society has generated an epidemic of acute and chronic anxiety which, when it affects the body, we call the "stress syndrome," a chronic state of tension and anxious worry that things will go wrong which keeps the sympathetic nervous system activated until it often becomes exhausted and collapses. Medical scientists tell us that stress can make us sick, physically and mentally.

Stress has been indicted as a causal factor in a wide variety of physical illnesses, from heart disease, hypertension, stroke, ulcers, asthma, and colitis to certain forms of cancer and immune system diseases. The chronic activation of the sympathetic-adrenal axis raises blood pressure and strains the heart, leading to cardiovascular disease. It also exhausts the immune system, which may increase the vulnerability to cancer. A new field has developed recently, psycho-immunology, which focuses on the effects of psychological stress on the immune system. So many people suffer from stress that stress reduction programs are common in hospital, clinics, schools, and industry. Stress has also been indicted as a cause or trigger of a wide range of mental and emotional suffering, from anxiety and depression to anorexia, binge-eating, substance abuse, phobia, paranoia, psychosis and suicide. Stress kindles the fires of anger, aggression, and violence.

The antidote to stress is relaxation and letting go. To relax when you are angry, you must first learn how to quiet yourself when you are not angry, and then apply what you have learned as anger arises. Since the energy of anger is fueled by the fight-flight reaction it can be tamed by turning the reaction down, calming the sympathetic-adrenal axis. This is known as the "relaxation response."

The relaxation response was first described by Dr. Herbert Benson, who measured the physiology of Buddhist monks in meditation. The physiology of meditation is the opposite of the physiology of stress, anxiety, and anger. In meditation, the heart rate slows, stroke volume decreases, and blood pressure goes down. Respirations slow. The muscles relax. The skin cools and the metabolic rate drops. The electro-electroencephalogram slows to the calm, attentive state of alpha rhythm. In sum, the sympathetic-adrenal axis is turned down. Experienced meditators can slow their heart and metabolism until they are in a virtual state of suspended animation.

Relaxation is an intentional turning down of the fight-flight reaction by means of a biofeedback strategy. The strategy has a physiological and a psychological component—relaxing the body and relaxing the mind. The two strategies work together. When the body relaxes the mind relaxes, and when the mind relaxes the body relaxes. It is not possible to have a tense body and a relaxed mind or a tense mind and a relaxed body.

Relaxing the body means relaxing the muscles. The tension produced by anxiety is muscular tension. The muscles are revved up for fight-flight with no one to fight and nowhere to go. You can learn the relaxation response by performing a simple procedure.

Sit down in a comfortable chair, close your eyes, and focus your attention on your body. To relax, you must first become sharply aware of the contrast between the feeling of tension and the feeling of relaxation. To do this, you can artificially create a state of tension by pressing your toes into the floor. Take your time and do it slowly and with awareness, pressing as hard as you can. The effort to press will create tension in the muscles in the bottom of your feet. Focus on these muscles. Feel the tension. Now, slowly let go of the effort and feel the muscles relax.

Tense them again. Let go of the effort and tense them again and again until you become clearly aware that *letting go of effort is the key to relaxing the muscles*. Intuitively, it makes sense. The tension of stress is effort without action. Stress is obstructed effort, obstructed desire, obstructed happiness project. The method for relaxing is very simple and direct: let go of all effort. Letting go of effort makes the desire moot. How can a desire be satisfied without effort? It's like flopping into bed at night and then wishing you had a cracker, but saying to yourself, "To hell with it (the desire). I don't want to make the effort." Without desire and effort, there can be no obstacles. What would they be obstructing? Relaxation is a letting go, not in the sense of going wild and crazy but in the sense of letting go of walls and barriers and opening to life as it is. Become familiar with this process. Be aware of the muscular tension. Let go of effort and relax.

Relax your body by letting go of effort progressively upward in each major muscle group. Once you have grasped the technique, there is no need to tense each muscle group before relaxing it. Begin with the bottoms of your feet then move up to your lower legs, upper legs, abdomen, chest, upper arms, forearms, hands and fingers, jaw, face, and brow. Visualize withdrawing effort from each group as if allowing a stretched rubber band to come to its resting position. Practice this regularly until you become skillful in letting go of effort in your entire body and relaxing into the present moment.

You may experience some resistance to doing this. Relaxation is threatening to the ego because it means letting go of your desires, your avoidances, and even of efforts to create and maintain a satisfactory sense of self. This can intensify feelings of personal and creature vulnerability and generate anxiety. Some people are too tense and restless to relax. They feel they must make an effort to be on guard in order to feel safe. Their stress is like a policeman protecting them from assassination. For these people, relaxing to reduce stress increases their sense of vulnerability and anxiety. This is a trap and the tragedy of stress. We feel it is necessary for the sake of our happiness to cling to our frustrated desires, while, at the same time, our stress (and unhappiness) consists of the fear that these desires will be frustrated. The linkage between a desire and the fear of its frustration gives stress a paradoxical and tragic aspect. Stress is, in part, the anxiety that without anxiety, without fear of the loss of what

we want, we will not get what we want and our world will collapse.
I often explain to patients that relaxing the muscles sets up a bio-feedback loop which turns off the sympathetic nervous system. It is the opposite of warm-up exercises. When we warm up we move our muscles by running, stretching, jumping, moving our arms, or doing sit-ups. When the muscles are activated, neuro-hormonal signals are sent to the hypothalamus to stimulate the sympathetic-adrenal axis in order to provide nutrients and remove waste products from the muscles. Exercise can relieve stress by metabolizing the sympathetic-adrenal hormones and the waste products of tension. Exercising turns the flight-fight reaction on (but without fear or anxiety). Relaxation turns it off.

Learning to relax is like learning anything. It has a learning curve. The more you practice, the better you will become at it. When you have become familiar with the strategy and method of muscular relaxation, and have practiced it when calm, you can apply it in a moment of anger. You can withdraw from the angry situation and relax until you are ready to deal with it. Or, you can relax while relating to the person or situation that provoked your anger. Be careful not to go into a relaxation trance while in the presence of someone you are angry at. It may aggravate the situation. Relax and relate. Train yourself to remember the simple motto: *"When anger arises, relax."* Remember this especially after you have reflected on the situation and decided that no acceptable alternative is available for the satisfaction of your desires. There may well be nothing you can do about anything. At that point, train yourself to open to the feeling of helplessness and relax. *The method is to be aware and accept the feeling of helplessness while relaxing the muscles.*

You might as well relax. You are feeling helpless because you can't have your way. Fighting the feeling of helplessness when nothing can be done generates feelings of vulnerability, tension, and anxiety. We get anxious not only about not having our way but also about feeling helpless. Accepting and opening to the feeling of helplessness soothes and calms the energy of anxiety and anger. It may seem paradoxical, but opening to the feeling of helplessness relieves it.

Opening to the feeling of helplessness means accepting it. Acceptance of a situation tautologically means not being anxious about it. Relaxing when anxious is not easy to do. With courage and practice, however, you will be able to find some inner peace even when times are tough.

The second practice is relaxing the mind. This is not as simple as relaxing the body. Animal or human, the body always lives in the present. When it is tense it is present. When it is relaxed it is present. The human mind has the capacity to be present but mostly lives in the imaginary spheres of past and future. We are constantly reminiscing and hoping, remembering past traumas and fearing future traumas. Discursive mind is a dream-weaver, a story-maker and a storyteller. It weaves the tales you tell yourself about yourself and your life. It is a problem solver. It sees troubles that have not yet happened, that might happen, and that might never happen. It thinks and worries and thinks, always about future happiness and danger. To relax the mind, this undisciplined discursive thought must be tamed and trained.

The traditional method of taming and training the mind is meditation. We have already discussed meditation (Chapter 3) as the method *par excellence* for developing awareness. Recall that the basic Buddhist meditation, shamatha, is also known as "calming" meditation, "calm abiding," or "dwelling in peace." This calming meditation is the basis of the relaxation response. The path of meditation is vast. The beginner must learn to calm down and pay attention. The intermediate must learn to open the heart. (See Chapter 10.) Some say that meditation is a path to enlightenment. About this I don't know. I have met many masters, and their most frequent response to inquiries regarding their own realization is to giggle or scowl, and deny that they are enlightened. They say that they are still working on it. They encourage us to keep working on it. It is an asymptotic process, continuous towards a goal but never reaching it. The masters say that meditation is difficult at the beginning and difficult at the end. We are all beginners.

As with relaxing the body, relaxing the mind requires a sharp awareness of the difference between a tense mind and a relaxed mind. A tense mind is a busy mind. A busy mind is thinking in the service of the ego. It constantly scans the life field, thinking about the past and the future, searching for ways to maximize pleasure, minimize pain, and protect, preserve, and expand itself. There is an old Buddhist saying: "A person with a busy mind is bound to suffer." This is because the evolutionary function of mind is to solve problems. A busy mind is a problem seeker, a problem finder, and a problem dweller. It is a worrier that dwells on its problems, generating a chronic state of anxiety and stress. A frightening thought can trigger a panic reaction. A tense mind is constantly triggering the fight-flight reaction in response to the dangers it predicts or imagines.

A relaxed mind is at effortless, attentive rest in the present moment, accepting the flow of events without self-centered judgment. Strictly speaking, it's impossible to think about the present moment. Now! Now! Now! It goes by too fast for linguistic mind to capture. By the time we have thought anything sensible about it, it is gone, replaced by another Now! Discursive thought stretches the present moment into a past and a future so it can grasp it, evaluate it, rejoice that it is consistent with our happiness projects, or worry that it is not. A relaxed mind is a silent, attentive witness of the dynamic present, where life takes place. A person who is relaxed into the present has "presence." Serenity and clarity are the fruits of the power of Now.

To bring busily hypermentating discursive mind into the present moment we need a rope and a hook, so to speak. The hook is our breath. It is present, in the moment, as long as we live. The rope is paying attention to the breath. Rest your mind on your breath. Breathe naturally. Follow the breath however it goes. Stay with it. Pay close attention as it rises and falls. Don't force even or deep breathing. Notice its frequency, depth, and undertones without commentary. When distracting thoughts appear, as they inevitably will within seconds, note gently and without judgment that you are distracted, and bring your mind back to rest on your breath and the gap between thoughts. Rest easily in these.

Beginners may be discouraged by how frequently distracting thoughts arise. Be patient. Even if you are able to pay complete attention to your breath for only a few counts, the practice of observing the cascade of thoughts, of gently releasing them and returning to the breath, is *in itself* a real accomplishment. Don't expect an immediate feeling of peace. Be with yourself in the present moment as you are. Meditation is a skill that requires practice to develop. Over time, with patience and persistence, you will gradually discover for yourself how to relax your mind into the present moment.

Relaxing means letting go. Relaxing the body means letting go of physical effort. Relaxing the mind means letting go of mental effort, including the effort to be happy. This is difficult for normal mind to grasp, so let us repeat. *Relaxing the mind means letting go of mental effort, including the effort to be happy.* Relaxation is a state of non-doing. Letting go means releasing your effort to figure out how to satisfy every desire, to avoid every distress, and to solve every problem. It means letting go of your happiness projects, if only briefly. It means dropping out of your biography. Forget who you are. You are just relaxed and attentive in the present—no one going nowhere. When practicing relaxation, try to be no one, with no life story, no preferences, just sitting and aware of the here and now. When you rise from your cushion you will be yourself again, with all your desires and anxieties.

In a Buddhist meditation called *tonglen* ("give and receive") we imagine giving away everything precious to us and taking in everything noxious to others. Give and take ride on the breath. Give on the out breath. Receive on the in breath. The purpose of the practice is to reverse the habit of normal mind to take in what is precious and to reject what is noxious. At first one simply visualizes breathing out light and breathing in darkness. This simple exercise is difficult for some people. Imagine a light at the center of your chest. As you breathe out, the light becomes brighter—brilliant. As you breathe in, the light dims and darkens.

Next you can imagine breathing out a sweet fragrance and

breathing in the smell of sewage. It is just an imaginary practice that softens normal, egoistic mind. The level of difficulty of giving and taking advances until you visualize giving everything you have to your enemy and taking all your enemies' burdens onto yourself. The final step is to take upon one's self the suffering of the world and give one's life in return. It may sound messianic, but remember it is not a happiness project. It is a practice for transforming our habitual selfishness into unselfishness.

In teaching this practice, I often ask people to *imagine* giving away everything in their bank account to a friend and taking on that person's debt. People struggle with this. I have been amazed at how many people find this difficult to do. They don't have to give away one actual penny! They only have to imagine it. But their attachment to money is so strong they become anxious at the mere idea of giving it away. The selfish self holds on tight to itself and to what it likes, and it avoids, rejects, or attacks what it doesn't like. Letting go is a healing reversal of this habitual pattern. It is a kind of alchemy that transforms vinegar into honey.

It is an unpleasant fact that the more strongly we hold on to our desires, our aversions, and our happiness projects, the more vulnerable we are to frustration, anger, and violence. This does not mean that we should let go of our happiness projects. We all need them. We humans need hope. Hope is food for the normal mind. We need hope that we can be happy in the future, or today will be gloomy. The problem is our attachment to our hopes. Strongly held hopes are no longer hopes. Hopes have an underside of uncertainty. It is like hoping red comes up in roulette. Strongly held hopes are more like demands. No alternative is acceptable. Letting go means loosening one's grasp on everything. Letting go means relaxing, simplifying, lightening up. It does not mean avoiding desires, avoiding hopes, or avoiding happiness projects. It means realizing that they are double-edged swords.

The paradox of hope is shown in the story of the man who was a God seeker. All his life he searched for God. He searched everywhere. Finally, in a tavern one night, he told his drinking companion about his happiness project. "You are in luck!" his companion announced with pride. "I know where God lives! I have His address!" The seeker went to the address and, as he approached the house, he had the happy thought: "All my life I have been seeking God and now I am going to meet Him. My fondest hopes and dreams will be realized."

He raised his hand to knock on the door when another thought arose, an anxious thought: "Now that I have found God what will I do for the rest of my life? All my life I have been a God seeker. What will I do now?" He dropped his hand and walked away with the answer to his question: "I will continue to seek God, but now I know where not to look." The man instinctively knew the importance of keeping hope alive. Oscar Wilde once said that there are two great tragedies in life. One is not to get what you want. The other is to get it. What do you do then? Raise another hope. Endlessly.

What to do with this dilemma? A fundamental teaching in all the esoteric traditions is balance. The basic principle of Taoism is that the universe is dialectical. At least two contrasting energies are required to establish a dynamic—*yin* and *yang*. Astrophysics says that the universe is composed of matter and anti-matter. Elementary particles have positive and negative charges. The primary motivations of living beings are attraction and repulsion, desires and aversions. The trick is to find the balance between antithetical extremes.

We think of mental illness as being caused by an imbalanced mind (or, in modern metaphors, by a chemical imbalance). One finds this imbalance in every form of so-called "mental illness," emotional suffering, errant behavior, and "craziness." What we think of as the sane mind is balanced between two extremes—for example, between hope and the acceptance of that which we cannot control. The balanced mind finds the middle ground between the wish to live and the inevitability of death, indulgence and restraint, action and passivity, selfishness and compassion, and so on. "The Golden Mean" and "The Middle Way" are teachings on balance.

In the olden days, Hasidic rabbis were like circuit preachers. They traveled from house to house on horseback giving teachings in return for food and lodging. After a meal, a host asked the rabbi: "Rebbe, how can we best please God?" The question really is, "How can we be happy?" because a basic, Old Testament article of faith is that God is pleased with the virtuous and rewards them with happiness and punishes the sinner with suffering.

The Rebbe answered, "I cannot tell you directly, but I can tell you a story." In the old days, accused criminals were forced to undergo a trial by ordeal. Once upon a time, two men were accused of theft by the king's agents and forced to walk a narrow beam across a deep gorge. If they were guilty, God would punish them with imbalance and death. If they were innocent, God would guide them across the gap. The first man walked gracefully across the beam to the other side. The second man yelled to him: "How did you do it?" The first man called from across the gorge: "All I can tell you is that when you lean too far to the left lean back to the right, and when you lean too far to the right lean back to the left!" That is the secret of happiness.

We find the same key teaching in Eastern wisdom tales. A devout Hindu asked his guru, "How should I practice my religion? Should I scrupulously follow all rituals, pray regularly, and obey every ethical command? Or should I live spontaneously and just let it all flow, like the masters seem to do?" The guru asked him: "What do you do for a living?" "I am a sitar player," the man answered. "And how do you tune your sitar?" The man thought for a bit about how to convey this musical task in words. Finally, he said: "Not too tight. Not too loose." "That's how to do it," his guru told him.

Balance is not a steady state. It is a dynamic process of continuous perception and decision. You can choose to lean to the right or to the left. You can choose to tighten or loosen. To transform the energy of anger, you can choose to let go of what you cannot have or cannot change. We have two kinds of choice. We can choose amongst the many things we want and can have. And we can choose how to respond when we can't have what we want. And, as the Serenity Prayer teaches, we can pray for the wisdom to know the difference.

At first, while you resist letting go and continue wishing for what you cannot have, it may take days after an outburst of anger for you to see the dynamic, accept the frustration, and relax. As you learn to let go of effort and relax into helplessness, the feelings of frustration and helplessness will gradually dwindle. Remember, the feeling of helplessness only arises in the presence of a frustrated desire. No desire, no effort, no feeling of helplessness. Over time the brief moments of letting go blend into a way of seeing your happiness projects differently—not as a matter of survival, or a matter of life and ego death. The wise know that any effort, any undertaking can succeed or it can fail. Success and failure are opposite sides of the same coin. The wise person is of like mind (calm, awake) in success and in failure.

This teaching is conveyed in a Zen story called "Is that so?" A monk was meditating in the forest when a middle-aged man approached him with a baby in his arms. "Monk," the man called angrily, "This is my daughter's baby! She says you are the father. So here. You take care of the baby!" The monk bowed, took the baby in his arms and said: "Is that so?" Five years later, the man came back. The monk and the young boy were quietly eating by the fire. "Monk," the man said, "I must apologize to you. My daughter has confessed that the carpenter's son is the real father of the child. She was ashamed to tell me five years ago. Now they have come together and want to marry and raise their child." The monk bowed, handed over the child, and said: "Is that so?" Few of us are so nimble. But even if we cannot achieve that heroic level of equanimity, there is always room for improvement.

If you take it steadily and slowly, you can learn how to stay relaxed whether things are going right or they are going wrong. When they are going right, relaxing is easy and pleasant, a brief pause. When things go wrong, when you are feeling frustrated, helpless, and anxious with no solution in sight, the only intelligent response is to relax and let go. When nothing can be done, do nothing. Just stay awake and aware of the changing inner and outer worlds. This will help you to develop the virtue of patience, the ability to tolerate frustration and pain without anger or aggression. With patience, the vinegar of your anger can be transformed into the honey of wisdom. If complete enlightenment is not possible, at least we can strive for a bit of it. The student asked the Zen master how to achieve enlightenment. The master replied: "Relax. Have a cup of tea."

10. *Step Seven: Opening the Heart*

THE SEVENTH STEP, the last step, is opening the heart. It leads us right back to the first step, as every ending leads to a new beginning. We return to where we started and see it in a new way, as if for the first time. In practice, all the steps are present in each of the steps. Sustain your awareness throughout. It will deepen your understanding. Take responsibility at every step. It will empower you to make wholehearted choices. Use your understanding to deepen your awareness and self-reflection. Bring everything you have learned to your decisions. After you have read and thought about Step Seven, start again at Step One. You will have a better idea of the way to go.

Opening the heart is not something you can learn from a book. It is a life process, a practice. We can't call it a happiness project except in a special way. It is a project to loosen one's attachment to all projects. It has been called "the golden chain." The "golden chain" is, in different forms, the desire to merge with God, or to achieve enlightenment, or, in this case, to open the heart. It is a chain because it is a desire and our desires are our chains, our bondage. It is golden because it is a noble desire. The desire to be free of bondage is itself a desire and can be a type of bondage. Metaphorically speaking, it is the last desire. Buddha used the metaphor of a boat (vehicle, *yana*) crossing a river. The boat is essential for the crossing. Once we reach the other shore (if anyone ever does) the boat, the desire, the chain can be dropped.

Pursuing our desires may bring us pleasure and transient happiness. Letting go of our desires may bring us peace and a sense of contentment. The trick is to find the balance. The paradox is that the very desire to open can close us. It can maneuver us into a false idea and inauthentic pretension of openness. In a sense, we can never know whether we are open or not because the very act of looking closes us. We look to check if we are succeeding or failing. Why else look? But how will we know? The outcome is likely to be either self-delusion or frustration. Opening the heart is not a kind of knowledge. It is a way of being in the world. The motto of the Karma Kagyu lineage of Tibetan Buddhism is "The goal is the path." It's not whether you win or lose that counts but how you play the game.

The desire to open the heart, like all desires, generates obstacles. The desire to open can make us dissatisfied with our condition of being closed and not yet open. We could become disappointed with ourselves and, to compensate, become heedlessly self-revealing, impulsive, and foolish. An irony worth pondering is that dropping the desire to open and paying attention to Now is itself an opening.

Another obstacle to opening the heart is the desire for happiness or some kind of bliss. We mistakenly assume that if we open we will be happier. Perhaps, but only if we define happiness as serenity and equilibrium rather than as getting what we want. We mistakenly assume that opening is the path to bliss. Opening the heart does not mean opening only to pleasure and closing to pain. To open the heart is to open to *every* situation as it is. If we are to transform the energy of anger, we must open to it. Opening the heart means opening to our anger and our pain as well as to pleasure. It means opening to frustration, failure, and death which we all experience. If we close to pain we must close to life because pain is a part of life; it is an underside to every experience, if only because everything changes. The Japanese have a phrase for the experience of life, *mono no aware*, which means "bittersweet."

If we close to pain we must close to other people, for they

may frustrate our desires. I recall a friend who thought that if he meditated faithfully every day he would become enlightened. He thought he would become wise, admired, and happy, a great achievement of which he could be proud. When his children or wife made noise while he was meditating, which happened regularly, he would rudely shout: "Keep quiet! Can't you see that I'm trying to meditate!" He became angry because they were spoiling his happiness project to let go of his happiness projects. Be prepared! The desire to open your heart will be frustrated by people and situations that threaten your deeply held desires and aversions. Regard these moments of frustration as opportunities to look into yourself more deeply and to respond more skillfully.

To know how to open your heart you must understand a closed heart. Open heart and closed heart do not, of course, refer literally to the physical heart. The heart is the metaphorical locus of emotion, intuition, and vitality. We Westerners live in our minds. We think in terms of open and closed minds. We regard a closed mind with disapproval as bad, as rigid, dogmatic, fixed, and resistant to new facts or ways of seeing. From the time of the Greeks, we have valued reason and logic as our guides to life. An open mind, we say, is reasonable and flexible. But whether the mind is open or closed, as Blaise Pascal observed, "The heart has reasons the mind knows not of."

It was once believed that the emotions were literally seated in the center of the body, just as we tend to believe that the mind is literally seated in the head. Some ancient cultures thought that the source of the emotions that move us is at our center, in the phrenum, the region of the heart and diaphragm where blood and air are in motion. The internal processes that support our being move in the center of our body, not in our heads. When we are emotionally wounded, we don't say, "my brain is broken"—we say, "I am heartbroken." We don't say, "I love you with all my head," or of a person who is full of life, "There is a man with a brain." The symbol of love is the heart, the wellspring of desire. The darkness of fear strikes at the heart. The life-protecting body armor of police and soldiers are bulletproof vests that shield the heart and lungs, the center of life. The Japanese locate the center a bit lower, at the *hara*, just above the belly button. *Hara Kiri* means killing the life energy—suicide. Opening the heart means opening to the center of our being and to the experiences of life.

A closed heart is marked by a habitual concern for one's self and one's self-interest—for one's desires, aversions, and ego. The idea of self-interest has the most profound psychological, social, and political implications. If we were to say that anger, aggression, and violence have a "cause," it would be self-interest. But self-interest is a very special kind of cause. Physical causality works from cause to effect. Psychological causality works the other way around, from the desire for an effect to a choice which, it is hoped, will cause it.

At the psychological level, everybody is selfish. It is given. Babies are born selfish, like animals. They need food, water, physical comfort, and security. They are "thinking" only of themselves, or, more precisely, they are aware of the world only in terms of experiences of gratification or discomfort. They are motivated by the life instinct, the desire to survive. Human action at all levels is strongly motivated by a self-interested, self-asserting, self-defending life energy.

We call the most extremely self-interested person "selfish" or "self-centered." He thinks and acts as if he is the most important person in the world. He is center stage. His desires come before the desires of others. We condemn people as selfish when they place their self-interests above our own. It is not a question of who is excessively selfish and who is righteously requesting consideration. We are being selfish even when we demand that someone else be less selfish.

One problem with self-interest is that the head and the heart are not always in harmony. In fact, the split between the head and the heart is a fundamental characteristic of human nature. The heart, seat of desire and emotion, often yearns for what the head, seat of reason and calculation, forbids. And the head sometimes bids the heart to endure what it fears and dislikes. The often-misunderstood psychiatric term "schizophrenia" refers to a radical split of thoughts and feelings. Thoughts which ordinarily are loaded with emotion are expressed flatly, without affect. Emotions erupt and quake with no corresponding (or comprehensible) ideational content. Head without heart is lame. Heart without head is blind. Opening the heart means finding an integral balance between head and heart. It is a matter of personal integrity. Another problem with self-interest is that our desires conflict—with the desires of others and with contrary ones of our own. The merchant wants to sell dear and the customer wants to buy cheap. Everyone wants the family car at the same time. We want relationship and freedom, merger and individuality. Humans are full of conflicts of desire. It is the essence of our universal neurosis.

Plato recognized that some desires are desirable and others are not. This distinction is the basis of ethics. The function of ethics, Bertrand Russell said, is to distinguish between good and bad desires and to promote the good. Socialization is a process in which individual self-interests are modified for the sake of common good. We cannot have sex whenever we want. We cannot punch or abuse people because they don't do as we want. We must mind our manners when we eat so as not to offend others with a display of brute appetite. We learn to be courteous to others to protect their fragile egos and our own safety. Opening the heart requires finding the balance between self-interest and the interests of others.

A closed heart is closed to the possibility of not getting what it wants, closed to the possibility of having to accept what it doesn't want, and closed to the idea that it is not the center of the world. Imagine the owner of a room, his own private room, who tries to collect and keep everything he wants in his room and to wall off and keep outside everything he doesn't want. In the same way, the closed heart builds a defensive wall around itself to keep the wanted in and the unwanted out. It wants to feel control over its life and environs and so, unwittingly, creates its own prison from which it then seeks release.

Having walled itself off from everything outside the room, the closed heart is closed to the complexities and ambiguities of life.

Things are black and white. Either I like it and I am for it and will let it in, or I don't like it and I am against it and will keep it out. The problem, as we have noted, is that dualistic mind projects antithetical qualities onto everything. Actually, nothing is completely positive or completely negative. All the people we love have both positive and negative qualities, virtues we admire and flaws we can't stand. Shall we let them in or keep them out? (Or keep them in when they are good and throw them out when they are bad?)

The closed heart is a lonely heart. It rejects the "not-me." This rejection manifests in all of our lives sometimes. Everyone, after a deep loss, a miserable quarrel, a painful rejection, or a humiliating public failure has felt the temptation to wall off the heart and never risk such pain again. Because life *is* so often painful, most of us develop boundaries and defenses that we hope will protect us from situations that might be intolerably hurtful. These boundaries and defenses must be porous, however, or we would be unable to connect to other people or open to life. Because we know that loved ones may leave us or die, and that our happiness projects may fail, we must decide whether to open to suffering or to encase ourselves within defensive strategies so tightly woven that our capacity for life and love is strangled.

Ultimately, at some level, the rejection of the not-me means being suspicious or rejecting of everybody. At some point in the development of the human individual, even mother becomes a not-me. The closed heart is haunted by paranoia. Closing to people leads to the feeling that they are rejecting you, even that they are after you. Why shouldn't they reject you? You have rejected them! And the more hurt they are by your rejection of them, the more they will be after you.

Groups of persons and nations also armor themselves against the potentially noxious "other" by identifying with their "own" affiliation group in antithetical relationship with everyone else's. This is the collective selfishness that manifests in blind patriotism, bigotry, racism, sexism, classism, and the prosecution of other as scapegoat. As in the individual, the tighter the boundaries that define the collective self, the deeper is the paranoia, isolation, and strangling rigidity.

The paradox is that the closed heart is also a social being. No one can live in a locked room without shutting down and closing to life. The heart yearns for intimacy with others. Sometimes it permits small openings, cautiously and to a degree, carefully controlling who and what is let in and who and what must be kept away. The problem is that once openings are permitted the wanted slips out and the unwanted slips in.

The closed heart is a state of strong attachment and is therefore vulnerable to feelings of frustration, helplessness, and anxiety which can ignite anger, aggression, and violence. Self-interest is the root. To the extent that our thoughts and actions are driven by conscious or hidden wishes, our hearts are closed.

Opening the heart is a direct antidote to anger, aggression, and violence. Opening the heart means centering, finding the balance between head and heart. It means letting go of what we want but cannot have, opening to the unwanted that we cannot avoid, and cultivating a sincere sense of humility rather than prideful self-interest. It means opening to pain—to feelings of frustration, helplessness, and creature vulnerability. And it means letting go, by degrees, of attachment to self, to self-interest, and to particular social identity. It means opening to life and to other people.

The positive side of our anger is that it gives us the opportunity to open our hearts. As we work with our anger, patiently and persistently, the cumulative effect is a softening of ego. It involves relaxing our defenses and gracefully opening to both the pain and pleasures of life. As we open to feelings of frustration, helplessness, and vulnerability, we tend to become less frightened of them, more willing to experience them, and increasingly able to relax into them. The effect is that we are more able to relax into our lives with a calm and tranquil mind.

It cannot be done all at once. It is a gradual and arduous process, but one which yields profound fruit. To open the heart means being an unrequited lover. It means grieving the loss of one's illusory hold on others, on the world, and on life while continuing to love them. It is a kind of surrender which is actually a victory—like giving in and apologizing, forgiving, or loving, rather than barricading oneself in a fortress of righteous resentment. It is opening to the bittersweet flavor of life.

A Tibetan lama friend told me a story about an experience he had with anger in India. He was a recognized meditation master as well as a graduate student in religion at Columbia University. We were discussing anger, attachment, and letting go. He had completed his monastic studies and was studying for a graduate degree in New Delhi. Having finished the final draft of his dissertation he took a train to visit friends in the north, bringing his only copy along. It was a hot, dusty day. At a brief stop in a small village, he got off the train to quickly buy a cold drink from a vendor at the station. When he returned to his seat his briefcase was gone along with his dissertation. He looked frantically for the thief but couldn't find him and had to board the train before it left.

He told me that, at first, he was angry. It is a natural reaction. Even the most advanced souls will sometimes get angry. The Dalai Lama, who as far as I can tell is totally without pretense, admits he gets angry. His admission that he gets angry reminds us that we all get angry. It's OK. It's what you do with it that counts. Pema, the lama, told me that his meditation practice helped him to quickly become aware that he was angry. He began to reflect on the spot according to his training. He realized that his anger was the result of his attachment to his manuscript. It was his happiness project, and it was gone. He could have remained in a state of attachment and desire, but he knew it would fuel his anger. To let go of his anger he had to let go of his manuscript, which in any case was irretrievably lost. So he let go. He told me his thoughts of the moment: "The thief must have been poor. Perhaps he was hungry. Perhaps he had hungry children. Perhaps he stole to feed his family or himself. If so, then my briefcase is benefiting him. Why should I be angry if some good comes out of my loss? I will let go of my manuscript. I gladly give it to the thief for his benefit. As I gave away my manuscript, my anger dissolved." He was not rationalizing. He was not playing "sweet lemon." He was using a technique to let go. He was not advocating that we excuse thievery or any other crime because the criminal may benefit. The moral of the story is that if you can't get what you want, then let go of it. If you lose something you love, then give it away. You might as well. You've lost it anyway and if you let go of it, you will lose your anger too.

As I've emphasized, developing awareness helps to open the heart. By developing awareness we can discover a quiet place within ourselves, an inner serenity from which we may see our self-interests and our anger more clearly. We may physically be in a serene landscape, a pond, woods, or the ocean, but if our minds are busy we do not have inner peace. We may be in a noisy city, but if our minds are quiet we have a sense of peace. We may not always be happy, but we can cultivate an inner serenity, calmness, and quiet which depends on our own efforts rather than on external circumstances.

Osho tells the story of a forest monk who interrupted a long retreat to visit his family in the city. As he walked through the marketplace, he was disturbed by the noise. Children were crying. Music boxes were blaring. Merchants were loudly selling their wares. Horns were honking. At first, the monk thought: "I can't stand this noise. I am going back to the quiet forest." As he turned and walked away, he had a second thought: "Wait a minute! Is the noise bothering me or am I bothering the noise?" He decided he was bothering the noise and continued walking peacefully to his mother's house. The lesson is that there is no point in "bothering," i.e., rejecting, fighting, or resisting, that which we cannot change.

By taking responsibility for our anger we open our hearts and transform ourselves. Instead of feeling helpless, confused, and agitated we gradually gain power, clarity, and peace. By developing self-discipline we gain power over ourselves–over our minds, actions, and emotions. We can feel good about this. We can feel tenderness and compassion for ourselves and true pride in an actual accomplishment. It is like the pride of learning to play the piano or giving up cigarettes rather than the false pride that is driven by the desire to be a great, powerful, meaningful person. Instead of pursuing happiness through the satisfaction of endlessly proliferating desires, we can let go and feel contented with ourselves right now, as is. More and more we find we can fully enjoy moments of bounty and good fortune and can remain tranquil in adversity.

As we grow more graceful in letting go of what we cannot have and in opening to the unwanted, we develop equanimity, a sense of inner balance. We become more confident that we can remain relaxed whether things go right or wrong. They are opposite sides of the same coin of striving for happiness. We win some, we lose some. If there is something that can be done, try it. If nothing can be done, relax and enjoy the victory of letting go of what you crave but cannot have and opening to what you dislike but cannot avoid.

To transform the energy of anger, aggression, and violence, we must honor the commitment to avoid hurting others. The world has not yet made this commitment. The world is dominated by the politics of the closed heart. If the Palestinians don't get what they want they will kill Israelis. If the Israelis don't get what they want they will kill Palestinians. If the Islamic extremists don't get what they want they will resort to violence. If their victims get what they don't want they will seek violent revenge.

Buddha, Christ, Mahatma Gandhi, and Martin Luther King were all champions of nonviolence. In spite of these saintly persons being almost universally beloved, a policy of nonviolence is a non-starter with most nations and many people. Why? Because nations and people are unwilling to relax their hold on their desires, their aversions, and their self-interests. In defense of their interests they claim to be right and righteous. In the international politics of closed-hearted machismo, softness is perceived as weakness. If there is a sense that desires are being frustrated, the unwanted is being imposed, and the sense of self-identity being diminished, the mood becomes one of helplessness, vulnerability, and shame. The futile, habitual response is violence and war.

What the world needs now is an ethic of the open heart. We must realize that we cannot have everything our way. We cannot have all the money we want. We cannot keep the riches of the earth to ourselves. We cannot have all the oil we want at the price we want. We cannot have continuous promise. There is no promised land. We cannot avoid pain, disappointment, and death. We cannot have all the freedom we want and we cannot avoid the restriction on freedom which is necessary for the common good. No one can rule the world because everyone wants to rule the world.

With the ethic of the open heart, you will be a more content person and the world will be a happier place. The open heart continues to search for happiness but lets go of what it cannot get or avoid. The open heart simplifies, gets down to basics, moderates desire, musters the courage to face the pain, and sees in the other a part of itself. Peace depends upon each side being willing to let go of something it wants and to accept something it doesn't want. The cumulative effect of opening the heart is a deeper understanding, appreciation, and sympathy for others. After all, we are all in the same boat. Everyone in the world seeks happiness and wants to avoid unhappiness, pain, and death. We all want to feel good about ourselves. We all experience frustration. We all become angry for the same basic reasons. An open heart weeps with compassion for itself and for others.